D1622674

Gavagai!
or the Future History of the Animal Language Controversy

LD
&CC The MIT Press Series in Learning, Development, and
Conceptual Change
Lila Gleitman, Susan Carey, Elissa Newport, and Elizabeth
Spelke, editors

Names for Things: A Study in Human Learning, by John Macnamara,
1982
Conceptual Change in Childhood, by Susan Carey, 1985
"Gavagai!" or the Future History of the Animal Language Controversy,
by David Premack, 1986
*Systems That Learn: An Introduction to Learning Theory for Cognitive
and Computer Scientists*, by Daniel N. Osherson, Scott Weinstein,
and Michael Stob, 1986

Gavagai!
or the Future History of the Animal Language Controversy

David Premack

A Bradford Book
The MIT Press
Cambridge, Massachusetts
London, England

This book was set in Baskerville by The MIT Press Computergraphics Department and printed and bound by Halliday Lithograph in the United States of America.

Library of Congress Cataloging in Publication Data

Premack, David.
    "Gavagai!" or the future history of the animal language controversy.

    (The MIT Press series in learning, development, and conceptual change)
    Bibliography: p.
    1. Human-animal communication. 2. Animal communication. 3. Languages—Philosophy. I. Title. II. Series.
QL776.P73 1986   599'.059   84-23155
ISBN 0-262-16099-4

Contents

Series Foreword

This series in learning, development, and conceptual change will include state-of-the-art reference works, seminal book-length monographs, and texts on the development of concepts and mental structures. It will span learning in all domains of knowledge, from syntax to geometry to the social world, and will be concerned with all phases of development, from infancy through adulthood.

The series intends to engage such fundamental question as

The nature and limits of learning and maturation: the influence of the environment, of initial structures, and of maturational changes in the nervous system on human development; learnability theory; the problem of induction; domain specific constraints on development.

The nature of conceptual change: conceptual organization and conceptual change in child development, in the acquisition of expertise, and in the history of science.

Lila Gleitman
Susan Carey
Elissa Newport
Elizabeth Spelke

Acknowledgments

I am indebted to Lila Gleitman, editor of this series, whose helpful comments first encouraged a manuscript to regard itself as a book. Dorothy Cheney and Robert Seyfarth kindly shared their erudition in animal communication with me, as did Phil Lieberman in the evolution of language (on those occasions when I have departed from his counsel, it has been at my own risk). Catch-as-catch-can conversations with Bill Labov on Walnut Street lighted more paths than he is likely to imagine. I owe a major debt to both Jonathan Bennett and Noam Chomsky for their four- to five-page turnaround replies to manuscripts I have sent them; their comments have been a mainstay of my continuing education. In this case as in all others, my wife, Ann James Premack, has generously showered the sparks of her mind on me. As a writer, she has spent years teaching me what a paragraph is, never faltering in her willingness to correct me in those cases where, owing to the "infinite novelty" of the paragraph, I still fail.

The research presented here has been supported by grants from the National Science Foundation. And "Gavagai" was taken, of course, from Quine's *Word and Object*, a classic that will engage readers for generations to come.

Gavagai!
or the Future History of the Animal Language Controversy

Introduction

In the early days of chimpanzee language research, colloquia on this topic often had the character of revival meetings. I remember three occasions when members of the audience rose midway through the official proceedings and launched unofficial colloquia from the floor. Despite differences in surface detail, the deep topic of these unofficial colloquia was always the same: man is unique. This content was the more remarkable because the official colloquium not only did not repudiate this claim but, when allowed to run its normal course, tended to reaffirm it in its own way. Yet for some, even to contemplate the possibility of language in a nonhuman threatened the claim of human uniqueness. The widespread supposition that by the end of the nineteenth century Darwin had largely cleansed the woods, at least in educated circles, was somewhat premature.

It was immensely foolish not to have anticipated the intense fervor this work would generate. Yet it was not easy to prepare for the occasion because so few other issues in recent academic psychology had had a comparable effect. The attention given the work by the media kept the emotion dancing. While most work in psychological laboratories proceeds without the slightest attention or diversion from the outside world, the chimpanzee language work was held continually before the public eye. This did little to quell the emotion and equally little, unfortunately, to maintain the quality of the work. For instance, it was not too long before apes were not merely talking but talking of past, present, and future (Patterson 1978). Although it is important, I suppose, for science to come into the media eye, once it does so (or endlessly seeks to do so, for all the blame cannot be put on the media), will it remain science?

The failure to have foreseen the uproar was a failure to recognize that any work bearing even remotely on a definition of "human nature" would have this effect. The controversy surrounding sociobiology is a case in point. As recently as the last century, the clergy defined human nature; today the role has been usurped by scientists, who have no greater consensus among themselves than did the clergy, and perhaps less.

The timing of the chimpanzee language work also added to the tempest. When the work began in the mid-sixties (Premack and Schwartz 1966), a return to rationalism had been under way in American psychology for perhaps a decade, hardly enough time for decisive victories but more than enough for border clashes and repeated skirmishes. Protagonists from both sides quickly made contact with the chimpanzee language projects. Behaviorists, who had been giving ground for a decade, now saw the chance to recoup all their losses in a single stroke, while mentalists saw not so much a scientific project as philistines at work.

A simply idiosyncrasy of American intellectual geography may have contributed to the tone of the controversy. To a Midwesterner the East Coast is an overheated place. Intellectual disputes in the Midwest are settled on intrinsic grounds. Cultural or sociopolitical factors intrude very little; the struggle is not one for power, and arguments come close to being settled in terms of the positivistic ideal. Not so on the East Coast. There intellectual disputes rapidly become political contests, and the number of adherents, the location of adherents in academic hierarchy, dialectical skill, connections with media, representation at international meetings—in short, power—play a role surprising to the outsider. At least this was true of the Midwest twenty or thirty years ago (it may since have been contaminated by coastal influences), but in my student days it was a naive or nonpolitical place, close to the Athenian ideal. The animal language controversy was not set in the Midwest, however, but in the East, which gave it all the stigmata of that intellectual locale.

The biologist was another participant in the sociopolitical entanglements of this research and ultimately a more important one than the behaviorist. During the period in which the dream of cognitive science became a reality (though the reality remained devoid of formal structure except for a small corner occupied by syntax), biology underwent a formidable growth through the combining of genetics and evolution. Sociobiology is the strongest of the ecumenical programs to have emerged from the neo-Darwinism produced by this combining of theory. It is unlikely to be the last, however, for the vigorous theoretical structure of biology is sure to cast off additional programs.

Biology could have allied itself with either protagonist—the dumb ape or the talking one. From one point of view, biology should be the natural partner of rationalism. Rationalism offers the first evidence for the impact of genetics on both body and mind: those mental structures that so preoccupy rationalism are not the product of experience but of genes. On the other hand, biologists are unequivocally committed to an unqualified continuity between human and nonhuman; and somehow when rationalists talk of language and of its uniqueness, they sound (especially to biologists) hysterical, like humanists (archenemies of continuity) rather than like scientists. Consequently, while the rare biologist (for example, Luria) sided with the rationalists from the beginning and a few others joined later (Monod, Jacob, cf. Piatelli-Palmarini 1981), the majority were immediately trapped by the issue of continuity and thus immobilized. They were never able to break free and reach more distance and substantive issues such as the genetic basis of mental stuctures. In the end, most biologists devotedly supported the ape—the talking one not the dumb one—which, as they saw it, is continuous with man.

Is the impression of missing linguistic links really a logical problem for evolutionary theory or only an emotional embarrassment, brought on by too simple a theory of evolution? What tenet of evolutionary theory says there must be intermediate links between animal call systems and human language? And what exactly counts as intermediate? Perhaps animal call systems are not even the appropriate place to look when seeking systems homologous to human language. Human language is after all not exclusively a communication system. The anticipated continuity may be better realized in conceptual structure, mental representation, not to mention perception. Moreover, there is no basis for anticipating a single measure of similarity holding for all the systems of related species. Notice that we are not in the least upset by the fact of missing links in quantificational ability, yet there is no doubt that the discontinuity between ape and human in quantificational ability is as great as it is in communicative ability. The one discontinuity disturbs us while the other does not. Why? How is this explained by evolutionary theory? The assumption of continuity, unfortunately, has in some respects more emotional than substantive content. When tangling with these questions about the evolutionary origins of language, I often found myself at a loss and looked to the biologist for aid, but seldom received any.

Neither did the linguist help the animal language inquiry in quite the ways that were needed. The questions for which one needed answers were very abstract: What is language? On the basis of what properties do we identify a system as language? The answers could emphasize either the structural or functional properties of the system, though the ideal answer would relate the two, showing the structures on which particular functions depend. By and large, linguists, concerned with the special properties of human language, did not address questions of this general kind. Not unreasonably, given their sense that human language is the only natural language to be found on this planet. But for the issue at hand, the idiosyncracies of human language are not entirely satisfactory.

Consider, for example: What is a question? request? description? command? promise? Human language contains all of these types and numerous others as well. The communication system of the bee does not. Is this a reason for discounting the bee's system as a language system, or are types of locutions a secondary consideration, not at all at the heart of what makes a system language? Suppose the ape could not be taught a system exactly duplicating the human one. Are there ways in which the ape's system could fall short and still remain interesting? Are there other ways in which failure would immediately disqualify the system, robbing it of all interest? In short, one needed a discussion of criteria that make a system language and even a weighting of these criteria. But discussions of this kind were hard to find, especially in linguistic texts.

The current proliferation of grammars—transformational grammar (Chomsky 1965, 1980), lexical functional grammar (Bresnan 1978), arc pair grammar (Johnson and Postal 1980), relational grammar (Perlmutter 1980)—might be seen as correcting this deficiency. Certainly this set of alternatives affords an enriched account of the structural possibilities. But notice they are all grammars of human "strength." We still do not have a set of grammars that could be arrayed along continua of structural complexity, complexity that could be translated into cognitive demands so that the system could be suited to species of varying resources. Of course, we cannot ask the linguist alone for such an account; the linguist and cognitive scientist must join forces. The latter must be able to advise the former what the realization of a particular structure would cost the species; how the species' resources would enable the realization to take one form or another; how the different forms might affect the several functions—truth claims, descriptions, questions, etc.—that the system would enable the species to carry out. In brief, we need at least a three-way relation, one connecting function to structure and one connecting this combination to resources. The pioneering effort by Miller and Chomsky (1963) relating embedding and right-recursive sentences to limitation on human short-term memory is an attempt of this kind. So, in a sense, is the recent work of Wexler and Culicover (1980)

and of Wanner and Maratsos (1978). For the time being, however, it may be just as well not to dwell on these matters; it
can serve little purpose beyond reminding us of how staggering
our ignorance is.

Although theoretical linguistics was not the guide one needed,
help did come from psycholinguistics through the study of the
development of language in children. For although children do
not have adult language, the system they do have was admitted
as language; admitted, because chilren appeared to have words,
units that they used somewhat in the manner of the adult word
and in time combined to form sentences (which again were not
like adult sentences). One of the embarrassments of this position
is the difficulty of stating what a word is. Nevertheless, the
problems confronted by those dealing with the acquisition of
language and the child's early systems were similar to those of
the ape language work, and the latter was helped by the former.
Indeed some researchers, the Gardners for example, proposed
to dispose of the whole question of what language is and how
we shall judge the success of the ape by simply comparing the
ape with the child. If the ape ended up doing what the child
does, it has language; otherwise it does not. This is an admirably
simple solution but unfortunately an untenable one. It has at
least two major weaknesses.

First, a merely technical one. The signing child is the appropriate party with whom to compare the would-be signing
ape, but the general account of sign is not only incomplete, it
is unfortunately most incomplete in the case of the child who
is acquiring or developing sign (although this lacuna is being
corrected by Newport and Supalla 1980; Bellugi and Klima
1975; and others). Second, and more basic, one cannot mean
literally "do what a child does" but only do the main or important
things a child does. "Literally" fails because there are numbers
of things children do that apes do not, and vice versa. For
example, although children occasionally sneeze while signing,
apes never do. Conversely, when signing in the presence of
food, apes are likely to grunt whereas children are not. To say

that criteria can be easily devised that would tag these cases as irrelevant impurities is to admit the need for such criteria, and the criteria become more difficult as we go along. For instance, in children facial expressions combine with hand signs to comprise grammatical distinctions, but they are not likely to do so in the ape because in the ape facial expression lacks full voluntary control and is largely reflexive (Chevalier-Skolnikoff 1976). Still more crucial, apes repeat signs, intrude extraneous signs into virtually all strings, and ignore order, at least to a degree not seen in children. Are these differences serious or are they too "irrelevant impurities"? To decide we must obviously have criteria, based, of course, on decisions as to what language is. Indeed, all the comparisons we make between child and ape will be based on decisions as to what is worth comparing; the fact that these decisions are often (too often) tacit does not mean they do not exist.

In addition to the general help that came from psycholinguists, special help came from American Sign Language (ASL). The study of ASL broke through the anthropomorphic barriers surrounding speech or vocal language, leading to attempts to find properties of language that held universally, independent of the physical medium of the language (see Klima 1975; Klima and Bellugi 1979).

In one sense, the animal language inquiry had more to gain from epistemology and philosophy of language than from linguistics. Reference, meaning, and truth are philosophical predicates, not linguistic ones. These predicates have the abstractness we are looking for and raise questions preferable to those of syntax, for the latter are ethnocentric and entangled in the special properties of human language.

In *Word and Object* (1960) Willard Van Orman Quine, using the context of translation, made a powerful examination of meaning, truth, and reference, which concluded that a field linguist encountering a genuinely alien language could not successfully translate or decipher the language. He would encounter insuperable problems. What then of the insuperable problems we must encounter in attempting to teach language to an alien species? Could we hope to establish glosses for the chimpanzee's would-be words or sentences?

We can, in fact, and as satisfactorily as we do with our language peers. Is Quine wrong, as mentalists have long maintained? Quine is wrong, I think, but not at all for the reasons mentalists hold. He has sold behavioral methods short: it is possible to make deeper analyses of meaning by strictly behavioral means than Quine has allowed for. So if Quine can be overturned, if the pessimism his position implies for the animal language inquiry can be lifted, it is not by mentalism but by a behaviorism stronger or more complete than his own.

For certain other philosophers of mind, the question of language hinges less on meaning and truth than on intentionality and belief. Probably the first question about a nonhuman's possible use of language that Grice (1975), Bennett (1976), and Dennett (1971) would wish to have settled is whether the use is intentional. By intentional they mean of course not only the speaker's intentions but also those he attributes to the listener, those the listener attributes to the speaker, those the speaker believes the listener to attribute to him, and so forth. Since intention is the most elusive (or unsatisfactory) of all mental concepts, it is no surprise that answering the Grice-Bennett-Dennett question poses extraordinary difficulties.

Yet the tools for answering the questions should be at hand, provided by learning theory and by social psychology. Both these fields have specialized in the problem of intention; but they have done so, it turns out, in restrictive ways that deny the problem a general solution. You believe that I have intentions and beliefs, and I believe that you have them. Are we alone in making these attributions? Do nonhuman species attribute beliefs and intentions to others? Regrettably, we cannot answer this basic question by calling upon either learning theory or social psychology.

We can expect no help from learning theory because, despite all the attention it lavished on expectancy (see Tolman 1932;

MacCorquodale and Meehl 1951; Irwin 1971), it was ensnared by instantiation and never reached attribution. Tolman et al. asked, "Do rats have intentions?" but never, "Do rats think others have intentions?" And it is, of course, the latter that must be answered if we are to decide whether, when a chimpanzee "speaks," he attributes intentions to his listener, his listener attributes intentions to him, and so forth.

Although social psychology was not entrapped by instantiation, it has never seriously considered any species other than humans (and in this sense, has no more biological basis than the humanities). In considering only human subjects, it has relied on what humans say and on what they believe, as this can be deduced from what they say. Social psychology, though preoccupied with attributions, has never asked what attribution might look like in creatures that do not speak. But to do justice to the questions of the animal language inquiry—and to the kind of analysis of intention that, for example, Bennett (1976) has offered—we must be able to show both instantiation and attribution (of intention and belief) in nonhumans. This calls for a new kind of evidence that does not and cannot consist of what the individual says. Ultimately we are forced to ask if the chimpanzee has a theory of mind (Premack and Woodruff 1978), and if so, how it compares with the human one. The issue of intentionality, like that of mental representation, is central to cognition; any attempt to give cognition a biological basis—to ask whether human mental life is continuous with nonhuman mental life—must address these problems.

Consider now two issues that might have played sizable roles in the animal language inquiry but in fact played no role whatsoever. The first of these is sign versus symbol or icon versus arbitrary symbol, distinctions that once held center stage in an earlier literature on language and communication (see Morris 1946). They were all but absent in the present controversy. This absence comments, I think, on the larger failure of would-be general communication theories—for example, systems theory (Bertalanffy 1968) or semiotics—to advance beyond their often elaborate prolegomena. But perhaps the development of these would-be theories only appears to be arrested. Perhaps their absence from the animal language controversy comes from the fact that the work is so unrelievedly of the laboratory. Real communication could not be expected to flower in so artificial a setting, and thus are general communication theories made to appear irrelevant. But fieldwork on primate communication has fostered no greater development of general communication theories. Why then should communication turn out to be a privileged biological function? Other biological functions, no less universal—respiration, digestion, excretion, reproduction, thermoregulation—have not proved to be sources of general theory. The proper question is not why communication failed to become a general science, given the rarity of this kind of development, but what might be the unique properties of those few cases on which we could mount a general theory? Obviously universality, or the widespread distribution of a phenomenon, is not a sufficient condition.

Symbolic play never became an active part of the animal language work, suffering a fate rather like that of the icon versus symbol distinction. In this case, however, the neglect is regrettable, for it is not unreasonable to link the development of language to a general representational competence; and symbolic play, when spontaneous, can be seen as an index of representational competence. Every intrinsic or innate competence has, I assume, an indigenous disposition for expression, one that is proportional to the magnitude or development of the competence. For instance, symbolic play is rare in the ape but common in the child, a difference that is proportional, I think, to the development of representational competence in the two species.

The discovery, which came out of the animal language work, that the ape does indeed have a representational competence, that it can be taught to judge the correspondence between a condition and a discursive representation of the condition, was foreshadowed by the discovery of symbolic play in the ape.

Köhler witnessed such play in his naturalistically caged animals (1925); the most vivid account is by Cathy Hayes concerning Vicki, a home-reared animal (1951); and we observed it in one of our laboratory animals, Sarah, an African-born, language-trained female. She had successfully reconstructed a cut-up puzzle of the chimpanzee face and then began transforming the face so as to give it a hat (Premack 1975); in this same period, she had observed herself wear hats in a mirror. Experiments then established that she did not transform the face except when she had the experience of wearing hats and that the kind of transformation she made was not invariant but could be affected by the content of her experience. After wearing hats, she applied a wad of clay to the top of the head, but after wearing glasses, she applied the wad to the area of the eyes and after necklaces to the neck or bottom of the face (Premack, unpublished data).

As to whether human language is species- and/or task-specific, one position holds that language did not develop from general intelligence but depends on a unique linguistic factor. Assume that this position is correct. It may still be the case that the unique linguistic factor appears in no species except highly intelligent ones. Indeed, how could it be otherwise? Suppose the linguistic factor were added to a frog or chicken, would we anticipate talking versions of these species? Symbolic play in the chimpanzee may tell us that this species has intelligence sufficiently developed—possesses those factors needed for language—to profit from the addition of a unique linguistic factor. Such a factor, however, does not appear to have been added.

Thus we need three positions in this argument, not the customary two. The issue is not simply whether language develops from general or specific factors but rather, granted that the factor is specific, what level of general intelligence must be present for the addition of a specific linguistic factor to be effective? We would not insist that language develops out of symbolic play (or a representational factor evidenced by such play); that claim, though common enough, goes far beyond the supporting evidence. But we would urge that adding the linguistic factor to a species that did not have symbolic play would be equivalent to wasting the factor. The general question of whether language is either species- or task-specific is one to which we will return in a final section.

Since the animal language controversy was blessed with virtually all the classic elements—genetics versus experience, language-specific versus general intelligence, rationalism versus empiricism—it could hardly be expected to have escaped having a red herring. The claims and innuendos of clever Hans were, of course, the fish in question (a fish that galloped more than it swam, however). That the claims were, in fact, a red herring and not those of a legitimate scientific issue could be seen in the makeup of the controversy from the very beginning. There are several forms the arguments would have taken had the debate been legitimate, none of which ever appeared in the repeated clever-Hans imbroglios. For example, no one pointed out that specific, reported, would-be controls for clever Hans were inadequate, noted what the inadequacy consisted of, and then suggested how to go about making controls adequate. Strangely (for a legitimate scientific discussion), no critic ever undertook to say what a proper clever-Hans control would look like. On the other hand, neither was it ever claimed that proper clever-Hans controls were simply not possible. Yet legitimate criticism must take either of these two positions. Of course, had the latter position been adopted openly, it should then have been necessary to explain how psychology at large had managed to survive, since of course it cannot be only apes that are subject to social cues but every living creature. Neither of these two substantive positions—the constructive one (what constitutes a legitimate control) or the nihilistic converse (legitimate controls are not possible)—achieved any prominence in the debate.

What is the actual frequency of social cues? Here is a simple procedure that can begin to provide an answer.

1. Select two tests that differ profoundly in difficulty (ideally one should be a test for which success is all but guaranteed,

the other a test for which failure is certain). For the chimpanzee or young child, these could be a simple match-to-sample problem and a problem that requires matching arabic numerals to their Roman equivalents.

2. Counterbalance the two kinds of trials in the same session.

3. Install your best clever-Hans control procedures, of course, and use an experimenter who knows the answers to both kinds of trials. Then test the subjects.

Suppose the results you obtain confirm your expectations; that is, the animal passes the one test and fails the other. You might then conclude that the clever-Hans controls are effective. There are other possibilities, however, such as there were no social cues to control. The trainer might not have transmitted social cues, or perhaps the animal did not utilize them. But we do not have to disentangle these alternatives; we are not attempting to assess the efficacy of the would-be clever-Hans controls, only asking a practical question: Are the results affected by social cues? To answer this, you have to take one additional step.

4. Repeat the original test exactly but remove all controls for social cues. Test the animal, in other words, as one tests a child.

Suppose the animal continues to pass the "easy" test while failing the "difficult" one; that is, the results for the sessions with and without controls for social cues are indistinguishable. These are exactly the results we obtained with Sarah, using the test material proposed earlier (object-match-to-sample for the "easy" test, matching of Roman and arabic numerals for the "difficult" test). Furthermore, we obtained these results with two different trainers (Premack and Wheeler, unpublished data; see table 1, page 156).

We do not know why we obtained these results (did the trainers not transmit social cues? did they transmit them but the animal not use them?). We do know that the thoughtful response to alleging that animals use social cues was to test for their actual incidence in research procedures. But nothing of this sort was carried out in the heyday of the research. Instead, polemic raged. For protection, researchers adopted (or were required to adopt) elaborate measures to control for social cues whose presence was never demonstrated.

In addition, the question that one most expected to hear over and over was somehow never heard at all: Why is a horse (given an indubitably unsolvable problem) a good model for an ape (given an arguably solvable problem)? Worst of all, legitimate and even interesting issues that do belong in this area rarely came to light, covered over as they were by the irrelevant. For example, there are in all likelihood species that have an intrinsic disposition to solve problems. A problem is not simply a stimulus condition, of course, but a condition that an individual recognizes as being incomplete (or in nonoptimal form) and then represents to himself as such. For instance, we can infer from Köhler (1925) that Sultan, his most gifted ape, often "saw" problems. Sultan watched from the sidelines with mounting agitation as his inept peers failed to perform acts he had already carried out. He threw off the restraints Köhler had imposed, rushed in, stacked the boxes, seized the banana, and then departed leaving behind the banana—uneaten. Members of some species strive to solve problems—to produce optimal configurations—simply for the sake of doing so, even when the effort is costly. For instance, when the rhesus monkey, after having solved a difficult problem, is given unsolvable versions of the problem, it quits responding even though rewarded for every response it makes (Pasnak 1979), indicating that the behavior of (even) the hungry monkey is not sustained by food alone and suggesting that there may be circumstances in which the monkey would exchange the opportunity to eat for the opportunity to solve a problem. Recognizing such dispositions helps us explain the persistent problem-solving behavior of the ape—the puzzling fact that many will fail to solve a problem despite deliberately conspicuous social cues (Premack and Premack 1983)—and places the clever-Hans issue in a different and proper perspective.

1

The Dolphin to the Rescue

In turning now to an evaluation of the research to which this controversy led, I shall lead off with the most recent contribution, an attempt by Louis Herman et al. (1984) to teach two dolphins a system that they liken to human language. The animal was first taught "words" for such objects as ball, frisbee, hoop; for such actions as spit, touch, fetch; and for such properties as bottom and surface. It was then trained to carry out commands combining these "words": ball spit, hoop touch, ball hoop fetch (bring ball to hoop), surface ball spit (spit at ball on surface not on bottom). Finally, the animal was given the usual transfer tests on new combinations of old "words" (ball touch, frisbee spit, frisbee ball fetch) as well as on new combinations involving old "words" in new locations in the string (bottom frisbee ball fetch). On the basis of successful transfer performance, Herman et al. attributed to the animal a finite-state grammar; thereafter, they speak freely of "syntactic categories," "semantic proposition," "lexical component," "syntactic rules," and the like. This flurry of linguistic terms is gratuitous, for to account for the dolphins' performance we need no linguistic terms of any kind.

Two rules will account for the whole performance: (1) (Property) Object Action and (2) (Property) Object Action$_2$ (Property) Object. Every performance carried out by the dolphins can be described as an instance of one of these rules: ball spit or surface ball spit as a case of rule 1; ball fetch or surface ball fetch bottom frisbee as a case of rule 2.

What is most notable about these rules, quite apart from their simplicity, is that they are framed in terms of categories that owe nothing to linguistics, that is, to an analysis of language. Object, property, and action do not derive from linguistic theory but have one foot in common sense and another in psychology. To the extent that these categories have been formalized at all, it is in perceptual theory and cognition. An individual knowing nothing of either "word" or "sentence" could walk through the world and point to examples of action, object, and property. The identification of members of these categories does not hinge on any linguistic analysis.

The rules of human language, in contrast, could not be framed in terms of such categories as object, property, action. Even the categories of semantics, agent, patient, recipient are, most linguists agree, inadequate. Human language requires syntactic categories—noun phrase, verb phrase, and the like. Consider the differences among these three sets of categories.

The first set is both the least specialized in domain and the least committed theoretically. The concepts of object, property, and action are perhaps as close to descriptive neutrality as human concepts are likely to come. For instance, action, which in the physical domain concerns the change an individual makes in the state and/or location of an object, can be identified largely without theoretical commitment, on the basis of behavioral criteria. The same holds true of object (cf. Spelke 1984) and property.

The semantic set, in contrast, is already both specialized in domain and theoretically committed. While an event can be identified as an action on behavioral grounds, the semantic concepts of agent, recipient, and patient of the action cannot be identified in this manner. To identify an individual as an agent, we must decide not only whether he acted, but also whether he acted intentionally, and this requirement applies equally to the other semantic distinctions.

The syntactic set departs further from the neutrality with which we began, not only in specialization of domain, but also in theoretical status. We can point to an action and even to an agent of an action, but we cannot point, except in a most indirect sense, to a noun phrase, verb phrase, or the like (though we could point to a unit of speech which on the basis of theoretical claims could be said to be derived from the categories in question). The categories of syntactic rules, rather than being definable ostensively, are defined explicitly by the roles they play in syntactic theory.

The distribution of these categories over species is a contentious matter. The best available evidence suggests the following: the "neutral" set will be found in all mammals, even perhaps all vertebrates; the semantic set to at least some degree in all primates (but in a well-developed form only in humans); and the syntactic set in humans alone. Loosely speaking, we may say the first set applies to the world, the second set to an interpretation of the world, and the third set to the mind of the interpreter.

Herman et al. have not yet arranged for the dolphin to produce language, and they would make a virtue of this weakness, claiming unusual advantages for comprehension. One might grant part of the claim if they would acknowledge that, however great the virtues of comprehension, adding the study of production does not detract from them. As the ensuing discussion will show, there are in fact several telling aspects of language competence that cannot be reached by comprehension (especially not comprehension of motor commands) alone.

Description of Self versus Description of the Other One

An appreciably more interesting form of language takes place when the ape describes both its own behavior and that of another individual. We can examine the two kinds of description and compare them. Although none of our three language-trained apes spontaneously described themselves, Elizabeth, an animal of average intelligence, came surprisingly close to doing so. Elizabeth's "training" consisted of little more than presenting items that were likely to bring out the behavior in question and omitting others that were likely to stand in its way. Specifically, we put Elizabeth in the presence of objects that would ensure free play—containers of water, a cutting instrument, a can whose suppressive lid invited insertion. To this, of course, we added her "writing materials"—the magnetic board and metal-backed plastic words that adhered to the board. We gave her a good supply of words but conspired to leave out those words that would have made possible her usual requests, specifically the word "give" and the trainers' names. Normally, in a situation of this kind, Elizabeth would have played for a bit and then made requests with her plastic words, asking the trainer for the fruit that was available.

She did play a bit, but almost immediately became restive, probably because she could not make requests. A highly excitable animal, she was just short of a tantrum when the "training" began:

The trainer pointed to the writing board. Elizabeth then wrote "Elizabeth apple." A moment later, she picked up the word "cut" but seemed not to know what to do with it, until the trainer again pointed to the board, whereupon Elizabeth added "cut" to the words already there, forming the sentence "Elizabeth apple cut." The trainer then gave Elizabeth a small piece of apple from the dish nearby and did so on all other occasions in the lesson when she made a complete sentence, whether it was an accurate description or not (Premack 1976, p. 90).

That was the full extent of the training.

Immediately afterward, she went on to produce 54 acts of simple play, 15 of which she "described." The play consisted of 20, 18, and 16 acts of washing a plastic apple, inserting it in the can, and cutting it, respectively. Directly following two of the acts of washing, three of the acts of inserting, and six of the acts of cutting, she "described" the act, writing "Elizabeth apple wash," "Elizabeth apple insert," and "Elizabeth apple cut," respectively. Her descriptions were 100 percent correct. On four other occasions in this lesson, she wrote strings of plastic words but they did not follow acts of play. Rather, they were themselves immediately followed by an act of play. One could say that these strings of plastic words predicted rather than described. In writing "predictions" she did something else she did not do in writing "descriptions": she combined the names of actions, writing for example, "Elizabeth apple wash insert." On this particular occasion she inserted but did not wash the apple, though she was correct on the other occasions, writing, for example, "Elizabeth apple cut wash," and then both cut and washed the apple. She was completely correct in her 11 "descriptions" and nearly so in the 4 "predictions."

The accuracy Elizabeth achieved in describing herself was not preserved in her description of others; nor was Peony, another animal of modest intelligence, very accurate in describing others. We arranged to give both animals acts to describe that differed from their own acts only in that they were carried out by another party. The trainers pretended to play with the same toys as the animal did, but their play was programmed, of course, and counterbalanced both the order and frequency of the three different acts of play (nonpsychologists may take this as a joke but psychologists will know better). In the first such test Peony correctly described the trainers' behavior, writing "Amy [Debby] cut [insert/wash] apple" on 9 of 15 trials, and Elizabeth was correct on 11 of 17. Both performances were above chance, as chance level for correctly selecting and ordering three words from a total of five is 1 out of 60.

Part of the difference between Elizabeth's accuracy in describing the trainer and in describing herself must lie in the difference between forced choice and a more natural use of language. In describing the trainer, Elizabeth was forced to describe every act, whereas when describing herself, she could "speak" or remain silent, choosing the acts she wished to describe. In remaining silent, as she did on 43 of 54 occasions, she could avoid occasions where uncertainty from any source would be likely to depress her accuracy.

Another part of the discrepancy, however, must have come from an entirely different source, one that is all too often overlooked in discussions of language behavior. In tests of free play, Elizabeth was found to have a preference order: wash, insert, cut. And this preference order could be used to predict Elizabeth's accuracy in describing the trainer. For example, Elizabeth accurately described all six acts of washing by the trainer (and wash was her preferred act); whereas she accurately described only one of five acts of cutting by the trainer (and cutting was her least preferred act) ($p < .01$).

Sarah: Synonymy, Relational Classes, and Conceptual Rules

In turning now to Sarah, a gifted African-born female obtained as an infant, we consider a different class of evidence, one that depends on the animal's ready ability to answer questions and to be at home with second-order relations (relations between relations). I would not say that this level of evidence cannot be obtained with less gifted apes, even Peony. Perhaps it could, but only if one were willing to divide each of the tasks into the smallest possible pieces and to instill them without regard to time or effort. With animals of Sarah's level of ability, evidence of this kind could be obtained with no more subdivision of task or expenditure of effort than could weaker evidence, with less gifted animals. Unfortunately, the difference between bright and dull is too often uninteresting. The brightest child counts "spontaneously," the next brightest can be taught to do so, and the child who is still less able can be taught only with difficulty. But differences of this kind do not teach us much, and they will not until we have proper theories of intelligence.

An act of description is of interest principally because of how close it comes to being a truth claim. In describing a condition—one's own behavior, the behavior of the other one, a static condition in the world—the individual arranges a correspondence or equivalence between a condition and a discursive representation of the condition. The properly ordered string of plastic words is the chimpanzee's form of discursive representation. The string of plastic words "Elizabeth apple wash" corresponds to the action that Elizabeth just carried out; "Amy banana cut" to the action that Amy carried out; "red on green" to a static condition holding between the red card and a green one.

The equivalence or correspondence that we recognize between the conditions and the strings of plastic words is what makes truth claims possible, no less in the animal's case than in the human one. The exact nature of this correspondence is problematic. As philosophical discussions of truth attest, the simple correspondence theory of truth (to which I have been appealing) gets into trouble, especially with respect to truth claims of mathematical propositions. The problems that correspondence theory encounters, however, come out of the complexities of human uses of language; they are not complexities that will arise for the ape. Correspondence theory may just be a perfect theory for a species whose possible uses of language can be no more complex than those of the ape.

The importance of truth claims or acts of description for our purposes is not philosophical but psychological. Acts of this kind presuppose the ability to do second-order relations or to make judgments about the relation between relations. The condition described is one relation, the discursive representation another, and the matching of one to the other is essentially a same/different judgment about the relation between the two relations. Since we already had evidence that even Peony and Elizabeth could match discursive representations to conditions, we took the next step—simple cases of synonymy, the matching of one discursive representation to another. For this we tried Sarah.

Sarah was taught to deal with equivalent sentences in three ways, each one more demanding than the other. First, she was given pairs of sentences and required to make same/different judgments about them. Next she was given only one test sentence and a set of alternative sentences and was required to choose the sentence that matched the meaning but not the structure of the test sentence.

Finally, she was given only one sentence along with a set of words and required to produce from scratch a sentence equivalent in meaning but different in structure from the test sentence (Premack 1976, p. 283).

After being trained in the three ways described—same/different judgments, selection of equivalent sentence, construction of equivalent sentence—she was given two transfer tests.

On the first . . . she was required to produce from scratch . . . sentences equivalent to the following: "Apple is red," "Red color of apple," "Brown color of chocolate," "Chocolate is brown," "Caramel is square," "Caramel is brown," "Square shape of caramel," and "Brown color of caramel." On each trial she was given six words drawn from the set "red," "brown," "apple," "chocolate," "caramel," "color of," "is," and "square," the only restriction being that the three needed to form the correct sentence were always included. She made two errors in 17 trials, none on the first five, or about 88% correct.

On the last transfer test of this series, sentences not used in any of the previous training steps were introduced. These included "Banana is yellow," "Grape is green," "Apple is big," and "Cherry is red." Two kinds of questions were given in a mixed order, one requiring that she make same/different judgments (Stage 1), and the other requiring that she answer with a sentence produced from scratch (Stage 3). An example of the former is: "Cherry is red? apple is red" (What is the relation between cherry is red and apple is red?), for which the alternatives were "same" and "different." An example of the latter was "Grape is green?" (What is equivalent to "grape is green"?), for which a representative set of alternatives was "green," "shape of," "color of," "grape," "brown," and "nut." She made 3 errors in 16 trials, 2 on same/different judgments and one on sentence production (Premack 1976, p. 287).

Although the sentences were physical entities, of course, in order to judge correctly between the two, she could not base her answer on the physical identity of the two sentences. "Apple is red" and "red color of apple" are not physically alike, yet she called them "same." In fact, they are less alike than "apple is red" and "apple is round," a pair she called "different." Nor could her judgment have been based on the number of shared words. Consider again "apple is red" and "red color of apple" versus "apple is round" and "apple is red." Each pair shared two words, yet she called one pair "same," the other "different." Nor could it have been based on shared word order, for "apple is red" and "cherry is red," judged "different," differ in only one word and not at all in word order, whereas "apple is red" and "red color of apple" differ appreciably in word order and yet were called "same."

To make same/different judgments about the pairs of sentences, as Sarah did, she must have represented the sentences not merely on a perceptual level, but also on a more conceptual or abstract level. This is not true for the comprehension of motor commands. If "spit ball," "touch stick," and the like were represented simply as perceptual events, this should in no way limit the animal's ability to respond to them. This holds for commands the animal is taught, but does it hold also for novel commands? Don't the transfer data, the animal's ability to respond to novel commands, require that the commands be represented on a more conceptual level?

We explain transfer by crediting the animal with having learned a rule, an association of some kind between categories (for example, action property object) and grant to the categories just enough abstractness to encompass the transfer data. The categories, however, are not instilled by the language training but are a part of the species' endowment; their abstractness is not in question. In question is whether the abstractness that applies to the categories holds in addition for the items instilled by the training, the individual "words" and their combinations. Notice that to recognize a command such as "spit ball" as an instance of the rule "action object" does not require that the command be represented abstractly; it could be represented merely as a sensory event and nonetheless be recognized as an instance of the rule. The synonymy data from Sarah, in contrast, concern the sentences themselves and provide rather direct evidence for the abstractness of their representation.

The evidence for abstract representation was corroborated by other data drawn from an unexpected and quite different source, pluralization. Although the singular/plural contrast is normally of only routine interest, the manner in which we happened to teach it to Sarah raised interesting questions.

Sarah was taught to pluralize by appending a *pl* particle to "is," so that "is + pl" was glossed as "are." The contrasts used in her training consisted of such pairs as "apple is fruit" versus "orange banana is pl fruit," "red is color" versus "red green is pl color," "pea is small" versus "marble cherry is pl small." She learned quickly, perhaps because the distinction itself is simple; furthermore, the *pl* particle that constitutes what Slobin (1983) calls a local cue is easily discriminated by children in language acquisition. It was not until after Sarah had passed the usual transfer tests, correctly pluralizing new cases, that I realized that the results were ambiguous: she could have been using either of two criteria, one intended, the other quite trivial.

For instance, in pluralizing, say, "chocolate caramel is pl candy," she could have been relying on the plural nature of the topic or merely on the physical fact that two words stood to the left of (actually above, since her sentences were vertical) the question mark. Which did she use? To find out, we had only to give her such sentences as "big apple? sweet" or "red apple? fruit," where the topic remains singular despite the fact that more than one word stands besides the interrogative particle. When given tests of this kind—actually the contrasts given her were more complex than these (see Premack 1976, p. 227)—her performance supported the conceptual rule. In 37 trials, she made only 6 errors (1 on the first 5), about 82 percent correct ($p < .01$). This outcome not only affirmed what we already knew, that she could learn conceptual rules, but also answered a question we had not previously asked. If given training equally compatible with a rule based on a physical distinction and one based on a conceptual distinction, which would she learn?

Although Herman et al. define *word* as "a unique independent semantic entity" (1984, p. 135), the reader should bear in mind how this abstract definition of *word* is actually translated by the dolphin experiment. A signal leads the animal to go, say, to a ball (rather than frisbee, hoop, etc.) independent of the location or composition of the ball. The dolphin instantiation of "unique independent semantic entity" is thus very different from the human's. A human word is, among other things, part of a system for representing information in the mind. The word is either an actual part of the information represented or serves as part of the system activating a natural discursive system ("mentalese"). This property is not the most easily studied, and it is doubtful that the comprehension of motor commands will ever contribute greatly to its study.

Similar considerations apply, of course, to *sentence*, where again Herman et al. provide both an abstract definition and experimental translation. In models of human sentence comprehension, a basic step is the identification of the grammatical class of the words (for example, Wanner and Maratsos 1978). There is, of course, no evidence at all for grammatical classes in the dolphin. Herman et al. recommend their work as a considerable methodological advance beyond the preceding ape language work. Perhaps it is. Its theoretical advance is another matter. The repetition of dubious claims made earlier for the ape hardly constitutes an "advance." Are we destined to hear similar claims for every species on which four to five years of "language training" will be lavished?

Teaching the comprehension of motor commands is a limited procedure, and no matter how cleanly executed, cannot do justice to certain topics—displacement and recursion, for example. Herman et al. describe a procedure in which they throw objects into a tank a moment after giving a motor command. Because a few seconds intervene between the command and the splashdown of the objects, the phenomenon is called "displacement." Even if hours passed, this would not constitute displacement. Displacement does not concern the individual's memory of the verbal statement; it concerns his knowledge of the world and his ability to use language to access that knowledge. A language-competent individual who knows about tigers, for instance, can answer questions about them even though no tigers are in view. Similarly, a language-competent dolphin who knows about the usual disposition of objects in the tank, or what a particular trainer normally wears, should be able to answer questions about these matters although they are not in view. It might be advisable to stop throwing things into the tank and concentrate instead on increasing the animal's language competence. If the animal could be brought to the point of understanding, for example, "If the hoop is where it was yesterday, then leap into the air" (or "Give this to the girl who wore the red sweater yesterday"), one could study displacement, even within the limitations of motor commands.

Their treatment of recursion offers another example of inadequacy. They give the animal not one command but two, and finding that the animal carries out both of them, call this recursion. Iteration is the appropriate term to use here. Recursion involves more than the simple repetition of an operation. A "problem" must be divided into parts and the same procedure applied to each part and to the products resulting from the operation on the parts. This gives rise to a hierarchical organization. In other words, the concatenation of nonhierarchical units does not produce hierarchy. In the misuses of "displacement" and "recursion"—as in the earlier uses of "word," "sentence," "syntax," and "semantics"—portentous terms are applied to inappropriate referents, falsely conferring on the dolphin those capacities demonstrated so far only in humans.

Stripped of all details, Herman et al. have shown two things: discrimination of temporal order and the learning of rules based on perceptual classes. Their discussion insists on a third: the discrimination of object classes (for example, hoop versus ball) despite broad variation in the composition of the classes. It is not clear why they favor this position. There is nothing demanding about the object classes they use, and surely there is no mammal that could not discriminate among them. Need we invoke mammal capacity? How about the pigeon? Recall pigeon success with the conceptually more interesting human, tree, water, and the like (Herrnstein et al. 1976). Moreover, though Herman et al. imply that the dolphin's success depends on language training, it could not be more clear that the pigeon's does not. Further, Herman et al. offer no evidence essential for their claim; they do not, for instance, compare the animal's ability to discriminate among object classes before and after language training.

Teaching language *could* have interesting consequences for an animal's ability to discriminate and classify items. The training might enable the animal to group items that it could not otherwise group, form superordinate classes not formed earlier, and combine and recombine items according to the changing criteria of language instructions. But none of these has been demonstrated so far in either the dolphin or the language-trained ape. Sarah was taught "fruit," "candy," and "breadstuff" (that is, cookie, cake, cracker, etc.), and she transferred these "words" successfully. However, we have every reason to believe that these categories were available to her beforehand (Premack 1976, p. 228). There is no evidence that concepts previously unknown to the animal were introduced by language or even that language served to sharpen the discrimination of existing concepts. Such claims lack the most elementary control: comparison before and after language training.

Confusing Conversation with the Mere Creation of Sentences

As part of his doctoral dissertation, Richard Sanders (1980) applied Lois Bloom's discourse analysis to a chimpanzee, Nim, that had been trained in ASL. From one point of view this was an apt move, for Bloom and her coworkers (1976) had begun to tease apart the complex and multiple changes that underlie the development of conversation in the child. And one could ask whether comparable changes were found in the language-trained ape. In examining the response children make to the speech of an adult, Bloom et al. noted first whether the child replied at all, and when he did, the form the response took. Their analysis is subtle and takes into account many distinctions, most of which are not germane to our purposes; we need only consider the main points.

The child either imitated some or all of what the adult said, did not imitate but retained the topic, or neither imitated the speech nor retained the topic. When he retained the topic, the child sometimes added to it, either preserving or modifying the structure of the adult speech. All these distinctions show interesting developmental changes. As the child grows older, he is not only more likely to respond to adult speech and to retain its topic, but also to expand on the topic, both semantically and structurally.

Although this gross summary hardly begins to do justice to the child's responses, it is already an enormous overrefinement of what is needed to describe the changes that Sanders observed in Nim. For as the first year of training turned into the second, and that into the third, the animal did not increasingly respond to the trainer. His signs did not preserve the topic of the trainer, nor did they amplify those of the trainer in any way. In fact, the animal showed only one change; he became increasingly imitative.

On the basis of these unrelievedly negative data, Terrace et al. (1979) drew a peculiar conclusion: the ape "cannot create a sentence," by which they mean cannot produce novel sentences. We have already seen, however, that not only gifted apes but also quite ordinary ones can "create sentences": ordinary ones by describing their own behavior and that of others, and a gifted one by producing sentences that are structurally different but semantically equivalent to other sentences. We may wonder whether Nim can do the same (the lesser task, the more demanding one, or yet another version of sentence production). But it is not possible to say from Sanders's data, for Bloom's discourse analysis is hardly a proper test. Conversation is a skill that goes far beyond that of producing novel sentences. Animals that never master the complexities of conversation may nonetheless create sentences.

Creating sentences is not one of the more demanding uses of language. To test the ape's ability to create sentences, we need do no more than invert the process of determining if it can comprehend novel sentences. But we must present new combinations not of words, but of nonverbal items. The combinations can be static (objects put into a container, one on top of another); or dynamic (the trainer or animal behaving in a novel way). Can animals produce strings that correspond to or "describe" these conditions? We have already seen that they can. Producing novel sentences is a weak use of language (especially when by "sentence" one means no more than is meant here, an ordered string of "words" exemplifying a rule framed in terms of perceptual categories).

Conversation, in contrast, is one of the strongest uses of language. One must first understand the speech or sign of the speaker and then reply with speech or sign of one's own. At a minimum, then, conversing requires not only the independent abilities to comprehend and produce, but also the ability to combine them in a particular way. For a more complete account of what discourse entails, we may return to the Bloom et al. analysis. To engage in discourse one must understand the give-and-take of conversation; be able to identify the topic of a conversation; be capable of amplifying the topic, semantically and/or structurally; and not least of all, beyond simply possessing these competences, be independently motivated to employ them (for the animal's training situation does not reward it specifically for discourse or engaging in conversation).

That the ape cannot "create sentences" is not the proper conclusion to be drawn from Sanders's data; perhaps the appropriate conclusion is that the ape cannot engage in conversation. Even that conclusion would need at least two qualifications. The first is a minor caveat. It turns out that Nim's performance is not a representative one; his tendency to imitate is probably the result of how he was trained. At least one other signing ape showed neither as much imitation nor an increase in imitation over the course of the training (Miles, forthcoming).

Perhaps, then, Nim failed to develop the more significant kind of changes shown by the child because these were blocked by imitation? No. We can rule this out by taking into account the other ape, whose training did not predispose her to imitation. She also did not show the systematic changes shown by the child.

The second caveat concerns the unclear status of conclusions drawn from data that are not merely negative, but are based on what an individual does spontaneously. To conclude from the Nim data that apes cannot converse, cannot learn give-and-take type rules, cannot identify the topic of a conversation, etc. would violate all the conclusions one normally draws about the difference between spontaneous performance and what an individual might be taught to do under optimizing conditions. The child, we know, is so programmed for language that only pathological deviations from normal environment will prevent its development. This is not the case for apes. And this holds not only for language but for many other aspects of cognition. For instance, feral apes give no suggestion of being able to do analogies, yet Sarah does them very nicely indeed (Gillan et al. 1981).

In the normal training situation, should the animal fail to identify the topic of a conversation (either because it cannot or because it can but chooses not to) and "replies" with a topic of its own, training does not come to a halt. On the contrary, the adroit adult quickly adopts the animal's "topic," and he is likely to do so each time his incompetent partner springs yet another topic from the blue. In this way, a sufficiently clever adult can give the impression of a conversation when, in fact, none exists, sometimes fooling not only the observer but even himself. The point is that since the animal's failure to preserve a topic does not terminate the lesson or cost it anything, the animal is neither rewarded for conversing nor punished for not doing so. Thus if any ape were actually to converse, it would do so strictly on the basis of an indigenous motivation to combine all the separate competences we have seen conversation to entail. This is the kind of motivation, or coupling of motivation and cognition, for which the child is justly famous, but it is extraordinarily unlikely to be found in the ape.

To examine seriously the possibility of discourse in the ape, we cannot rely on spontaneous performance but must take the usual didactic approach: analyze discourse (as Bloom et al. have done), identify the simplest acceptable exemplars, divide them into components or atomic elements, and then seek training that will instill the pieces and bring them into the desired configuration. By a happy accident, we have already done this to some degree for one of the components of discourse: identification of the topic.

In the earliest stages of Sarah's training, we often gave her only two alternatives to choose between. But once she achieved a lexicon of from twenty to twenty-five "words," we routinely offered more than two alternatives:

From about this stage of the training on, we regularly added five to ten irrelevant words to any set of alternatives given her on a production test. . . . The attempt to increase difficulty in this manner was of doubtful success. The records show that Sarah never used an irregular word. . . . Most of the . . . sentences germane to each lesson . . . made up a well-defined set. The boundedness of the lesson . . . could not but have helped Sarah *discover the topic of the lesson* (Premack 1976, p. 126, italics added).

Evidently, then, the ape can "discover the topic," provided of course that the conditions of discovery are sufficiently simple. Are the conditions in question too simple, making the ape's "discovery" trivial? They may well be, but then we must ask whether there are ways to amplify those too-simple conditions without at the same time losing the ape. In these accidental findings we have the tempting possibility of leading the ape from a trivial performance into one of greater interest.

Given the visible limitations of the language-trained ape, why would anyone bother applying the Bloom et al. discourse analysis to such an animal? Whoever imagined that apes could converse?

In fairness to these writers, one must recall that there was a period during which extraordinary claims for apes were commonplace (not that they have disappeared entirely). No one was more responsible for these claims than the Gardners. The impression left by their work is that the language of the signing ape and that of the signing child could only be differentiated through close analysis. Indeed, in one study they found the ape superior to the child (Gardner and Gardner 1974)!

In that particular study, the Gardners examined the replies of the ape Washoe to *wh-* questions and claimed to find evidence for grammatical classes. Unfortunately, the study is flawed both methodologically and substantively. The methodological flaw, as Seidenberg and Petitio (1979) pointed out, was that the Gardners' record of the animal's response to a question was seldom equivalent to the animal's actual response. For instance, "You me you out me," the actual sequence produced by the animal, was recorded as "You me." The signing pattern of the ape, characterized by repetition, intrusion, and irregular word order, was "edited." Is this really as devastating an error as many suppose? What the Gardners appear to have assumed is something like: if *we* can extract from the ape's garbled message what the ape is trying to say, so can the ape. Of course such an assumption needs to be made explicit and, more than that, tested. Quite how to test it in the case of sign is not clear; using plastic words, the test is more easily accomplished. The clumsy pieces of plastic may themselves be helpful, for they are likely to slacken the manic speed of the animal, the famous chimpanzee impulsiveness.

Suppose we remove from the animal's supply of words those that permit repetition as well as others that are probable sources of intrusion. Further, suppose that when aided in this manner the ape does produce cleaner signals. This result would indicate that the "noise" in the ape's signing reflected a performance rather than competence failure and that not only the human but also the ape understood the message in the garbled response.

There is, on second thought, a test using signing that could make the same point. We could offer the ape a choice between "listening" to the trainer produce those clean, orderly signs he normally produces or noisy, irregular ones like those the animal produces. If the ape were to show a preference for the clean signals, it would seem comparable to the child who, though unable himself to produce correct forms, recognizes them when they are produced by others. Occasionally, young children provide marvelous examples of such disparities. At a stage when the child himself mispronounces various words, he will vigorously reject adult mimicry of his phonetic errors (while at the same time accepting with perfect equanimity adult pronunciation that may differ drastically from his own). On the other hand, if the ape were to fail all tests of this general kind, then the methodological criticism would be very telling indeed. It would indicate that clean signals and clear messages do not exist in the ape's mind at all. They are strictly a construction of the experimenter.

Even if we give the methodological point the benefit of the doubt, the substantive problem remains. The Gardners' claim of grammatical classes is based upon the *wh*- question and is borrowed from an analysis proposed by Roger Brown (1968). In adult speech, the formation of *wh*- questions supports standard linguistic models with their customary reliance on grammatical classes. But what is shown by the formation of such questions is not shown merely by answering them. One might learn to answer *wh*- questions simply by associating with each *wh*- marker words of a perceptual kind: for example, names of individuals with "who," places or locations with "where," objects with "what." The formation of such associations would make no syntactic demands whatsoever, and indeed the whole ability to answer *wh*- questions would then reduce to a "discrimination learning task" (Seidenberg and Petitio 1979). In fact, the Gardner data did not concern the production of *wh*- questions but dealt only with answering them.

Language and Transfer

For the sake of convenience, we call the animal's acquisition of rules based on perceptual classes "language" and the training resulting in such rules "language training." But the need for caveats is immediately obvious. Labels recommended for the sake of convenience establish neither that the language bears any resemblance to human language nor that the learning is in any way special.

Consider, first, the learning. Is the learning shown by the ape or dolphin distinctive, different from what we might anticipate in lesser (or smaller-brained) species? Is it a kind of learning that moves these creatures closer to the human? At long last are we finally in a position to disclose how the learning of intelligent species differs from that of those not so intelligent?

The distinctive feature of dolphin performance may appear to be that of transfer. Trained to associate, say, stick with fetch and ball with touch, the animal applies fetch to ball and touch to stick. But transfer per se does not distinguish this from any other case of learning. Any individual trained to fetch one object or touch another will fetch or touch objects different from those on which it was trained. Similarly, an individual trained to fetch or touch objects signaled by distinctive stimuli ("words") will respond to other objects signaled by the "words" associated with them. Whether it will respond to all objects (all things "that move in unison") or only to objects encountered in the training locale or merely to objects physically resembling those used in training is difficult to predict. The boundaries of transfer are generally discovered, not predicted, and may vary with the species, the training conditions, or even the individual. Irrespective of species—rat, ape, dolphin, or bee—no individual forms associations strictly between training items alone; the association is always between the types of which the training items are tokens. All learning has this character. Skinner (1935), among the first to observe this fact, formulated the stimulus and response as generic or class concepts. It would be interesting, therefore, to have the dolphin experiment carried out with other species, especially those species not lauded for their intelligence. In part the procedure has been carried out with the sea lion (Schusterman and Krieger 1984), but the results for rats and pigeons should be especially informative.

The First Round of Data

Suppose a monkey or child, trained to respond to a particular triangle, say, an equilateral one, is given three basic tests. Consider now the tests and their predictable results. First, the child or animal is required to choose between the equilateral triangle and the other triangles (independently rated for their similarity to the training triangle) and to do the same for the rest of the series, choosing between the most similar triangle and the others, etc. No surprise, he chooses the training triangle over the others, and the remaining triangles in proportion to their similarity to the one used in training. Second, he is given the same set of triangles, one at a time, with reaction time recorded. He responds most quickly to the training item and to the others in proportion to their similarity to the training item. Third, he is given a standard transfer test: each triangle is pitted against a circle, square, rectangle, etc. He chooses all the triangles—not only the equilateral but also the right-triangle, isosceles, etc.—over all the nontriangles.

In the third test, we speak of transfer (rather than generalization) because the data demonstrate an equivalence class. In the competition between triangles and nontriangles, all triangles are equal. But are they? In fact, they are not, for, as demonstrated by the generalization data, an individual chooses one triangle over all the others and chooses it most quickly. Although triangles constitute an equivalence class, experience claims its prerogative: one triangle is special.

Let us consider the parallel between "generalization versus transfer" of the animal-learning tradition, and "identification procedure versus core concept" of the human-concept tradition. Using the latter distinction, George Miller and P. Johnson-Laird

(1976) accommodate a number of "odd" facts: people have a preferred instance of odd number (Armstrong et al. 1983), find one instance of bird to be more birdlike than another (Rosch 1975), sometimes identify "grandmother" on the basis of experienced attributes (grey hair, plump, facial lines) rather than by formal definition. Odd number, bird, grandmother constitute equivalence classes (as do triangles); furthermore, members of these classes that are actually experienced will enjoy special status (no less than the equilateral triangle of the example above). Intension/extension, sense/reference, core concept/identification procedure, transfer/generalization—this series of largely isomorphic distinctions, generated by different intellectual traditions, defines a central property of concepts that can be found in nonhuman species, including quite primitive ones.

Consider Aplysia, an invertebrate most recently initiated into the "club" of species for which learning has been shown. When its mantle is shocked, the Aplysia retracts it. Furthermore, the Aplysia can be conditioned to so respond by the pairing of shrimp concentrate with electric shock (Carew, Walters, and Kandel 1981). There is little doubt that now a change in some feature of the shrimp concentrate will produce a weakened conditioned response—generalization. But if we can produce generalization we can also produce transfer (although to do so may require weakening our procedures to accommodate the creature's primitiveness). Let us propose this as an equivalence class: any shrimp concentrate, no matter how dissimilar from that used in training, will produce a stronger response than will any "nonshrimp" concentrate. In substituting response magnitude for choice, we do not violate the basic idea of an equivalence class. We then have both the basic ("first round") conceptual phenomena in an invertebrate; that is, items in the class are equal compared to items outside the class, and experienced members of the class enjoy privileged status. These data of the "first round" are all but inevitable: they scarcely distinguish human from mollusk; they appear with the dawn of the concept of concepts.

The Second Round

Differences, if there are any, are more likely to appear in the second round of data. The second round derives principally from a single fact. In using the triangle once again as our equivalence class, we find that while all triangles continue to be chosen over nontriangles, items resembling (not themselves actually) triangles are chosen over nontriangles. For instance, a two-sided triangle will be chosen over a square—even over a three-sided square (the definition of triangle as "three-sided" notwithstanding). This leads to puzzlement concerning the status of, for example, tigers without stripes, three-legged cats, cats without whiskers or meows, for these definition-defying creatures would still be accepted as tigers, cats, and the like. It also inclines some to talk about "essences," the essence of cat for example, which may or may not be preserved under varying transformations of cat. However, if there are essences, these will, as Hilary Putnam (1975) and others have indicated, vary according to the viewpoint of the individual, in particular the point of view of the expert. And since the knowledge of experts varies from year to year, so will essence. A nonimmutable essence makes a very poor essence.

What appears to be at stake, more than "essence," is mental reconstructibility. An individual will accept as cat (tiger, triangle, etc.) any portion (or deformation) of cat (triangle, etc.) from which he is capable of mentally reconstructing a normal cat (triangle, etc.). This suggests that we pursue the principles of mental reconstruction, taking into account, of course, how these vary with items as different as grandmothers and triangles. Notice that I do not attempt to say what cat is or how it is mentally represented. In view of the observable progress, I am content to leave that problem to others (see Smith and Medin 1981 for a comprehensive discussion of these issues).

The second round of data has to do, then, with the fact that an equivalence class cannot be stated as simply as I had suggested. Items resembling triangles, tigers, birds, etc. but not themselves any of these things will nonetheless be chosen over nontriangles, etc. Does the second round of data differ, then, from the first? Do we now have species differences? Certainly, to some extent. We do not look for mental reconstruction in the mollusk. But vertebrates? and especially mammals? It would be a great surprise to find mental reconstruction confined to humans.

2

Learning, Hard-wiring, and Cognition

Neither in the phenomenon of transfer nor even necessarily in the kinds of categories needed to account for the transfer does ape or dolphin learning differ from learning in general. On the contrary, it continues the long tradition in which the study of learning has steadfastly refused to disclose interesting systematic differences among species. Jeff Bitterman (1975) could take exception to this claim, but in a sense his own work is the best argument against such an objection. By ingeniously showing, for example, incentive shift in the bee (the bee, among other things, buzzes "angrily" when shifted from a high- to a low-concentration sugar), he has eliminated a learning paradigm that might have distinguished the invertebrate from the vertebrate (1982).

It must be admitted that Bitterman has found species differences, as has Passingham (1982, p. 126). Passingham reports an orderly relation between the evolutionary status of the species and the amount of interproblem transfer shown in the learning-set paradigm. This is the kind of monotonic ordering one has always hoped to find, and it is, of course, a perfect example of what we would mean by a quantitative rather than a qualitative or fundamental difference between species. The differences that Bitterman reports are more difficult to interpret. For instance, painted turtles demonstrate improved reversal discrimination learning but mouth-breeder fish do not; the turtle thus resembles the rat in this case. Fish do not show incentive shift but, as noted above, bees do. What parameters in the learning model can these differences reflect? Are they fundamental? These questions are not easily answered, nor is a general learning model simple to construct (see Estes 1969; Rescorla and Wagner 1972 for seminal attempts). If the process of learning has undergone fundamental change from its probable inception in the invertebrate, it is not yet possible to give an account of those changes.

Learning and Hard-wiring

Whether or not species differ fundamentally in the basic process of learning, they may well differ in other processes. The two principal alternatives to learning are cognition and processes attributable to hard-wiring (for brevity I will drop the "attributable to" and speak only of hard-wiring). Because of our present state of ignorance, it is hardly a cut-and-dried matter to distinguish the three cases of learning, cognition, and hard-wiring; but it is a challenging matter and worth a try.

The study of language acquisition in the child affords an unusually rich opportunity for attempting to isolate and compare the three processes. Opportunities for comparison are especially good during periods when the child is reorganizing old forms because these are periods well-known for their sudden influx of errors. Preceding these periods, the child produces certain forms fluently, with apparent knowledge. During these periods, however, "feet" becomes "foots" or "feets," "cut" becomes "cutted," "melt" incorrectly becomes "unmelt"; and such contractions as "don't" and "can't," disappear as the child substitutes uncontracted forms such as "can not," "do not," and the like. These changes suggest that the child's initial correct usage was based on superficial knowledge, piecemeal rules, unanalyzed forms—a general failure to recognize the higher-order relations among the individual forms. In the period of reorganization, the child analyzes the "unanalyzed" and connects the "unconnected," often over-extending the results of his new "discoveries." Reorganization, once regarded as influencing only a limited aspect of language, that is, word changes or inflectional morphology, is currently regarded as a broad process affecting virtually every aspect of language. Reorganization, in Melissa Bowerman's colorful phrase, "flows continually beneath the more overt signs of progress like a subterranean stream" (1983, p. 319).

Inflectional morphology found in speech provides some of the simplest examples of reorganization, and recent work by Lissa Newport (1983) gives examples of such reorganization in American Sign Language (ASL). Newport found that signs have a morphological system, a layered or shell-like arrangement. The center of the shell consists of a "root," which is the main source of meaning. Immediately next to the root are derivational morphemes coding grammatical class, such as verb to noun (paint/painter). The outer layer contains inflectional morphemes coding such distinctions as tense (walk/walked) or number (painter/painters). Newport gives an enlightening account of how the child penetrates the shell to the root, acquiring the morphological system. I offer only one adjustment to her account. She attributes the entire process to learning. While I would agree that part—the very beginning as well as the very end—is due to learning, the interesting part of the process is not learning but hard-wiring. Indeed, if that process is not an example of hard-wiring, then we are not ever likely to find hard-wiring in the human.

The process starts with learning. The child's first task in acquiring language is to compile a data base consisting of word-meaning associations. At this stage words undergo no internal analysis; they are holistic, phonological entities. Despite the lack of analysis, the child's use of words is fluent. For example, he uses both irregular (foot/feet) and regular (dog/dogs) forms on appropriate occasions. But he has no rule of pluralization and his success is owed to the classic mechanism of learning. He has formed associations between each of the unanalyzed words and the stimulus conditions.

This structure, a compilation of unanalyzed word-meaning pairs, is exactly the structure provided by learning. The language case differs from more familiar examples because of its magnitude. We encounter learning in the invertebrate (where learning appears to have originated) and are therefore accustomed to a simpler version: individual stimuli and/or responses are associated. The process occurs on a large scale, perhaps never larger than in the child's acquisition of language. But sheer numbers of associations do not change the basic process. Holistic or unanalyzed items are associated, each pair essentially independent of any other pair.

More interesting is the next stage, where hard-wiring appears to enter. When the word-meaning pairs are in place, a "window opens" in the child's mind, and a process that seeks to achieve the simplest possible description of the data base is set in motion. We may wish to assign the process a more powerful goal, that is, not merely to describe the data base but to reproduce it as well. Any process capable of finding the rules that will realize this possibility must differ from the simpler process required to produce the initial data base.

In acquiring the data base, the child adds word-meaning pairs one by one. But regularities in the data base cannot be detected by looking at the word-meaning pairs one by one. To find the regularities, a distributional analysis across at least some part of the entire data base is required. Minimal pairs must be found—words that differ by one unit only, such as paint/painter, paint/painted, paint/paints. The search for minimal pairs must be guided by hypotheses. What distinctions in meaning pair with what parts of the word? The hypothesis that, for example, "ed" marks tense and "root + ed = past" will be either confirmed or refuted by the regularities unearthed by the distributional analysis. Finally, the process must distinguish nouns from verbs or it will mistakenly pluralize verbs and add past tense to nouns.

The kind of representation that is needed for performing a distributional analysis goes well beyond what is needed for learning. Even if we were to grant that conditioning (even in Aplysia) requires in some sense a representation of the CS and US—the shrimp powder and electric shock—the representation would be comparable to that of short-term memory. Different indeed from the ability to represent the whole data base in long-term memory—precisely the capacity needed for performing a distributional analysis. Indeed, the quality of the representation needed for distributional analysis would automatically exclude some species. For instance, although invertebrates learn—react "appropriately" to individual experiences—if there were patterns in their overall experience, invertebrates would be unable to detect them. Morphological rules are associations, but of a kind different from that between CS and US; they are formed by a process different from and appreciably more complex than that of conditioning.

When the distributional analysis is complete, learning enters once again, now to establish associations between morpheme classes and stimulus conditions. It is entirely possible that a refined analysis of meaning has accompanied the phonological analysis—for example, the concept of past (see Bowerman 1983) or even plural may change. The evidence on the stimulus side is more elusive, however, and will not be pursued here.

There may be some reluctance to accept morpheme-meaning associations as examples of learning. There may be even more reluctance to accept rules formed by the morphological analysis (that is, "root + ed = past") as attributable to learning. As matters stand, what is currently called "learning" is notoriously unspecified. There are constraints on neither the kind of "linkage" that counts as an association nor on the kind of "items" that can be associated. An alternative is to attempt to constrain learning in one way or another. Here I have chosen instead to leave learning unconstrained and to differentiate among species by adding (to some species but not to others) processes that stand between perception and learning. In simple species, perception (even sensation) is the only "analysis" available; there are no intermediate processes and learning operates on the immediate content of perception. In humans, learning operates on perception as well as on outputs from any other processes (such as distributional analysis) that stand between perception and learning.

Can we imagine learning in a nonhuman that would have the slightest resemblance to the child's acquisition of inflectional morphology? In a dog perhaps? Suppose we train a dog to turn left to one tone and right to another. After the dog learns the auditory problem, we add a visual one, attempting to teach the dog to go up for one light, down for another. But not only does the dog fail to learn the visual problem, its performance also collapses on the auditory one. The dog's errors are not random, however. It never responds up/down to tones or right/left to lights, but behaves as though it has made a higher-order (though mistaken) generalization: tones go with the horizontal dimension, lights with the vertical. Finally, in a third phase, the dog both recovers the auditory discrimination and learns the visual one, evidently "correcting" the higher-order generalization.

The association of dimension and modality—with a resulting transient period of error—is somewhat analogous to the child's performance. The child correctly contrasts "foot/feet" and "dog/dogs," but later, observing the similarity between "feet" and the far more common "dogs," produces "feets." Our hypothetical dog differs fundamentally, however, from an actual child. The dog's accomplishment, a combination of cognition (higher-order generalization) and learning, seems exceptional. But all children, not just the exceptional ones, make a distributional analysis. Cognition is not combined with learning. In the child hard-wiring is combined with learning.

Creolization
Children not only extract the morphological system of normal language, but, to some extent, also construct a morphological system when the language environment is abnormal and does not contain such a system (Bickerton 1984; Sankoff 1980; Slobin 1977). The child is shown to be a creator (not merely an analyzer)

of language by two "experiments of nature," both of which denied the child exposure to a normal first language. In one case, he received pidgin as his first language and in the other what is called "frozen" sign.

Pidgin is an impoverished language invented for purposes of trade or commerce by two adults who do not speak the same language. Words in pidgin tend to lack inflectional and derivational morphology. We could anticipate, for instance, "give" but not "giver"; "give" but not "gave"; "give" but not "gives." Pidgins resemble the artificial languages taught to apes (including the use of a syntax based entirely on word order). In frozen sign (Fischer 1978; Newport 1982), those signs that normally vary in shape and location (providing the inflections that change meaning) remain unvaried, as in pidgin.

Children who receive impoverished inputs (like the above) as their first language add elements to the system. By adding inflectional morphology and a more elaborate syntax, they upgrade the pidgin to a creole. They appear not only to turn pidgin into creole, but also frozen sign into normal ASL (Newport 1982). At least this is true for children who receive impoverished inputs before their sixth year. Do children who receive pidgin after the age of six enrich the received data base? Or continue to speak pidgin? That natural experiment seems not to have been fully observed; but the sign or ASL version of the experiment has been. Many deaf children receive frozen sign as the first language after their sixth year. These tend to be first-generation deaf children—children of hearing parents. They receive delayed exposure to sign, because of an emphasis on speech. These children contrast with those who receive frozen sign early. They retain the original system into adulthood.

Rules, Conventions, and Scientific Laws: Task and Species Specificity

Is the distributional analysis species and/or task specific? Although not confined to speech—as Newport's example nicely shows—it may yet be both task and species specific, that is, confined to human language. But we need to broaden the inquiry to do justice to this topic. We have been concerned here with one case—rules (for example, root + ed = past)—while ignoring two others—conventions and scientific laws. We must now compare these three cases to clarify the general nature of hard-wired analysis and to show what constrains such analyses and why they tend to be both species and task specific. But first let us be clear about the three cases and the differences we find among them.

Rules of language, the only kinds of rules we are considering here, are demonstrated clearly by the examples given. Sweden recently provided a remarkable example of a convention: on a given day, at an appointed time, all moving cars stopped and then resumed, driving on the opposite side of the road. As examples of scientific laws, any number will serve—the gas laws, one of Newton's basic four, Hooke's law, and so on.

The profound differences in these three cases are best demonstrated by examining human attitudes toward exceptions. An exception to a convention is regarded as illegal, and the individual who engages in such exceptions is punished. Exceptions to language rules, in contrast, have a special status, and members of a linguistic community are expected to observe them. It is only the ignorant who fail to do so. Exceptions to scientific laws have yet another status. Nothing worse can happen than to find exceptions to a scientific law. One must show that the exception is bogus (not really an exception), that it can be excluded on principled grounds (thus changing the boundary conditions of the law), or one must be prepared to give up the law. Exceptions are thus dealt with very differently in the three cases: punished, honored, or denied. How do we happen to observe or, as the case may be, discover these three kinds of regularities?

Conventions, we say, are learned. The rules of language, in contrast, depend in only small measure on learning; learning merely prepares the way for hard-wired processes that actually extract the regularities. Scientific laws offer yet another contrast.

Although every child "discovers" the rules of his language, only a few turn into adults who discover scientific laws. Finding scientific laws depends far more on cognition than do either conventions or rules — at least defending the laws against threatening exceptions depends heavily on cognition. The initial discovery of such laws remains a mysterious process, however.

We now ask the interesting question: Could scientific laws (or conventions) ever be extracted by the same hard-wired analyses that "discovered" the regularities of language? We can answer this question best by asking two other questions. What conditions make it possible to acquire rules in the case of language? Could these conditions be realized outside language, in particular in either science or convention?

In the case of language, there is the need for two conditions: a data base and a procedure capable of extracting the regularities contained in the data base. We recognize this "recipe" in the Wexler-Culicover model (1980), which, of course, is a model for syntax not for inflectional morphology. Can we foresee realizing (or arranging) these conditions in either science or convention?

Try to conceive of a set of observations from which to arrive at the gas laws, Newton's laws, or any other physical law. Can we conceive of a procedure which, given the data base, would arrive at the regularities contained within? Let us finesse the second question by simply assuming a positive answer. The human brain could instantiate the needed procedures — some obviously already have — if given the right data base. So, perhaps, could the brains of other species, especially if assisted by well-defined or strong data bases. This assumption assures a prompt return to the first question, where the real interest lies.

In the acquisition of language, the data base is derived from the behavior of the species. For instance, the child hears sentences in conjunction with nonverbal conditions. These sentence-condition pairs make up the data base in the Wexler-Culicover model and correspond to the simpler word-meaning pairs making up the data base in the case of word morphology (actually, the data base in the former consists of the sentence plus a base phrase marker that is itself derived from the child's nonsyntactic comprehension of the sentence-condition relation). In both cases, the complex no less than the simple, the regularities contained in the data base are embodied in the actual behavior of the species. Every normal child who acquires language has at least one caretaker who converses with him, at the same time observing certain relations to the environment. The caretaker does not, for example, merely turn on the radio and close the nursery door. In those rare cases when this does happen, the child does not acquire language: for there is a limit as to how weak the data base can be. Pidgin, for instance, may be impoverished, yet it provides a strong enough data base for the extraction procedures to operate. But what of a caretaker who, though wonderfully affectionate, never addressed the child in sentences (only spoke to it in word-utterances)? We rarely encounter such aberrations; fortunately, the genetic makeup of the species virtually assures every normal child a caretaker who will embody the needed regularities.

In considering the gas laws, for example, or food taboos in the case of conventions, arranging for species-specific behavior that would embody the needed regularities becomes a problem. Admittedly, it may be simple ignorance that makes these cases appear difficult. I have not yet been able to derive the possible sets of observations from which the gas laws (or any other laws) might be extracted. Until this is done, it is senseless to speculate on the matter. Let us, instead, assume that it can be done. If so, and the needed data bases are embodied in the experience of the species, then there is no reason why scientific laws (and conventions) could not be acquired in the same way as language. But suppose they were. Would we not then greatly change our attitude concerning exceptions in these cases?

Surely, yes, for there would no longer be proprietary rights over laws—no "Newton's" laws, for example, or "Hooke's" law or "Boyle's"—only laws that belong to the species. And exceptions to regularities extracted by hard-wired analyses on data, guaranteed by virtue of species membership, are bound to be viewed differently than exceptions to regularities discovered by the cognition of one individual.

It appears that the sense of personal responsibility (conventions) and achievement (scientific laws) depends on a particular blend of learning, hard-wiring, and cognition. What if the human "blend" were changed, the amount of hard-wiring greatly increased? It might very well gravely threaten our present evaluation of individual responsibility and achievement.

Cognition versus Hard-wiring

We see the data base as the product of learning and the distributional analysis as the product of hard-wiring. But why hard-wiring? Mental representation of the data base (plus computation on that representation) sounds exactly like cognition; indeed it appears a perfect fit for the most common view of cognition. Of course, we could insist that the computation is automatic (rather than conscious and intentional)—which is, I think, quite correct—but it would be regrettable to force this distinction on concepts which, in their own continued struggle for legitimate scientific status, are more needful of help than helpful. Following are four grounds, of a more operational kind, on which we might distinguish hard-wiring from cognition.

One, both the distributional analysis and the constructive processes of creolization appear to occur within a restricted period of the child's life. The window, which may open after two years of age, appears to close before the age of six. The assumption of a critical period may help to explain the impoverished, or incomplete, language acquired by the victims of Down's syndrome. Lenneberg (1976), with characteristic prescience, held that Down's children acquire language in a normal sequence, but more slowly—and then stop early. Ann Fowler's more recent data (doctoral thesis, 1985) refute only one of Lenneberg's three claims; she finds the rate of language acquisition normal. This suggests that in Down's syndrome the problem comes from the fact that the window closes too early.

Two, the distributional analysis may have a minimum triggering requirement, whereas cognition seems not to. We can tackle one physics problem or a series of them. This is not a matter about which we presently know a great deal: individual differences may be important; analysis may be triggered by different amounts of data, lasting for different durations; and different degrees of systematization may be achieved by different individuals. My suggestion is simply that ordinary cognition does not require a minimum data base. We can use cognition to do "little" tasks or big ones; hard-wiring may well be confined to "big" tasks.

Three, the command to *stop* may differentiate the two processes even more revealingly than the triggering requirement or command to *start*. What stops the child's acquisition of language has always been a mystery. Is it the lack of time that prevents the child from discarding normal adult syntax and moving on to a more elegant system? If the closing of the window could be delayed, would the child produce (or seek to produce) more powerful language systems? For instance, would a child reanalyze the same system, adding or dropping rules if, after the child had already analyzed an earlier input, we provided a changed data base? Since human words have two layers, and the bilingual child analyzes two layers of each of two languages, could he also analyze four layers of one language? Does the child "stop" because he has exhausted the regularities, run out of time, or achieved as much of a system as he was able? Cognition, in being tied to motivation, differs from hard-wiring. A stubborn individual may dash himself repeatedly against a data base (that just as stubbornly refuses to disclose its regularities) while at the same time cutting short his efforts on other problems (thus using quite different standards on different problems). Hard-wiring behaves differently; it does not seem to fail as cognition often does, perhaps because it is triggered by only those data bases that guarantee at least some level of success. Cognition alone tackles problems whose solutions are in doubt. On the other hand, if hard-wired analyses did fail, how would we ever know? We may be the graveyard of a host of failed hard-wired analyses.

Four, the child may be unable to carry out, as isolated cognitive acts, computations that are an integral part of the overall internal analysis. For instance, analogies could be part of a morphological analysis. The analysis might find, say, hit/hitted analogous to kill/killed, leading to the kind of error that marks reorganizational periods. But the same child may be unable to solve comparable analogies when they are presented as isolated problems. A satisfactory version of this point obviously depends on the identification of components of the hard-wiring process; for the time being, it is no more than a guess or prediction.

I have not sought to differentiate hard-wiring from cognition on grounds that they consist of a different set of computations. I assume that the set is the same in the two cases, or at least that every computation in the cognitive set has a hard-wired analogue. It seems to me that all the "ideas" of cognition must come from the hard-wiring, by a route that is presently mysterious. Thus, the hard-wired set may be larger than the cognitive, containing members to which cognition has not yet gained access (see Rozin 1976 for a comparable idea). A difficult assumption to test, obviously.

Learning versus Hard-wiring

Consider as an example of hard-wiring the device responsible for the acquisition of language. Can we distinguish a device of this kind from that of conditioning or learning? The most common connotation of hard-wiring as "innate" will not help to differentiate the two cases because learning and language acquisition are both innate. The phrase popularized by Harlow (1949), "learning to learn," may suggest otherwise, but we find the phrase to suffer under close examination.

Recall our earlier definition of learning as a process in which, under specified conditions, one item is associated with another. By substituting this definition in the phrase "learning to learn," we obtain this claim: associating one item with another (under specified conditions) improves the ability to associate other items with one another (under specified conditions). That is, we emerge with the claim that conditioning can be conditioned.

The animals on whose data this claim was based were subadult and adult monkeys (Harlow 1949), a population that would have formed many nontraining associations prior to the specific laboratory training in discrimination. For example, if we estimate the average number of associations an individual forms in a day at ten (a moderate estimate), then a monkey that begins discrimination training at three years of age would have a repertoire of over ten thousand associations before its introduction to the laboratory. That is, the formation of associations does not begin in the laboratory! After the formation of ten thousand associations, can additional associations increase the rate at which new associations are formed? While the monkeys reached criterion (on successive discrimination problems) in ever fewer trials, it is doubtful that this can be attributed to an improvement in learning. The benefit to learning is better attributed to non-learning processes: the elimination of competing responses and the acquisition of new strategies, for example. Estes and Lauer (1957), by estimating changes in the "learning" parameter of Estes's model over successive trials, reached a similar conclusion.

If we could change the definition of learning to something other than "the formation of associations," we might discover a process better able to account for the acquisition or improvement of itself, thus making the phrase "learning to learn" a sensible one. Or we might yet find an acquisition process (altogether different from that of learning) that would account for the acquisition of learning. Until either of these alternatives is realized, it seems preferable to regard learning as an innate process that is little modified by experience.

To distinguish hard-wiring from learning we will need to find some basis other than innateness. Learning (as we have treated it here) is a general-purpose device. It stands in contrast to hard-wiring processes, those special-purpose devices designed to provide specific competences such as language, music, mental maps, numerical computation, and possibly face recognition. We observe this contrast not only on the output side (the adult competence provided by the device), but also on the input side (the conditions that trigger the device). As an example, let us compare the conditions that trigger conditioning and those that trigger language acquisition.

Presumably, there are many kinds of inputs that do *not* trigger language acquisition. The food eaten by the child does not specifically activate the language-acquisition device (although food does activate conditioning since foods properly situated in a fixed sequence are subject to association), not because such foods lack all regularities or even because they lack the regularities the language-acquisition device is designed to detect. (Grammars attempting to describe the composition and sequence of meals have been proposed, in fact.)

What does trigger the language-acquisition device? Unfortunately, the simplest answer, speech sounds, cannot be correct. They are not a necessary condition because, as experts in sign assure us, the grammar of sign does not differ from that of speech (Klima and Bellugi 1979; Newport 1983). The device must therefore be activated by sign as well as by speech. Nor can speech sounds be a sufficient condition. Children cannot acquire language (it is widely agreed) from speech sounds alone. A child whose only contact with language consists of daily readings from the encyclopedia (the "Brittanica experiment," Premack and Schwartz 1966) will not acquire language; speech must be paired in some fashion with nonlanguage scenes.

The Wexler-Culicover (1980) language learnability model suggests one possible trigger or effective input for the language-acquisition device. In this model, pairs consisting specifically of the base phrase marker (*b*) and the surface structure (*s*) of a sentence enable the child to infer the transformations mapping the base phrase marker to the surface structure. This trigger is quite obviously tied to one view of adult grammar, Chomsky's transformational view, and would have to be revised (probably, along with the inference process itself) to accommodate alternative views. But for our purposes this model has the virtue of showing how specific the trigger must be for a special-purpose device to yield a specific output. Of course, this conclusion could be reached on far simpler grounds. A device constructing mental representations of space must be capable of extracting specifically metric properties from the other properties describing a space. Similarly, a device that recognizes faces, if there is such, would have to be capable of distinguishing faces from nonfaces.

Let us consider that the b, or the base phrase marker of the Wexler-Culicover model, is part of a trigger mechanism. In contrast to the surface structure of the sentence, b is not given to the child directly, and consequently the child must construct the base phrase marker. Wexler and Culicover assume that the child, though without syntactic knowledge, can do so simply from knowing the words used in the sentence and understanding the situation in which the sentence is uttered. They are encouraged in such a view by Slobin (1979), who examined a large body of speech that adults directed at two- to five-year-old children and concluded that the children could understand the sentences without any use of syntax. They merely needed to know the words and understand the "normal relations between actors, actions, and objects."

This view of "pre-syntactic sentence comprehension" encourages one to regard the acquisition of language as a two-step process in which the steps are profoundly different. For instance, only the second of the two steps is hard-wired. Triggered by the bs pair, it leads to the construction of adult grammar. In contrast, the first step is based on a general-purpose device, learning. It consists principally of the acquisition of words. Actually, the first step must also include the comprehension of thematic relations—for example, action, actor, object—and the acquisition of this competence. Such comprehension is far more problematic than is the acquisition of words. We cannot claim that the thematic relations are learned, for there are no primitives from whose combination we could derive "action," "actor," "object," or the like. Such thematic concepts, as all other concepts, must simply be granted the child—an ungratifying, unilluminating, yet unavoidable conclusion.

The two-step model may be especially appealing to those eager to give the language-trained nonhuman its linguistic due. They will willingly concede the second step to humans, if the first step can be granted to nonhumans. Unfortunately, however, we must be wary of granting the first step to nonhumans, for there is virtually no evidence that the sentence comprehension of nonhumans is based on the comprehension of thematic relations.

Cognition and Learning

In those species that lack cognition, learning can affect (and be affected by) only learning processes. For instance, if we have produced conditioned leg flexion in an individual, say, by pairing tone with shock, we can then affect the original learning either by extinction (tone no longer followed by shock) or by counter-conditioning (tone now paired with food). But in species that do not lack cognition, the learning process can be affected by belief and/or knowledge; that is, a system that lies outside of learning can influence the process of learning.

Of course, in humans learning can be produced by verbal, no less than by perceptual, information. "When the tone sounds, I will deliver a light shock to your arm" is as effective in producing conditioning as is the actual pairing of tone with shock. Conversely, "when the tone sounds, I will no longer deliver shock to your arm" produces extinction equally effectively (Brewer 1974). But the production of learning through such instruction provides better evidence for linguistic competence than for cognition per se. Direct evidence for the effect of cognition on learning can be achieved without any language instruction.

For instance, suppose we apply a Bechterevian procedure to dogs as well as to humans, pairing a tone with shock to the foot (resulting in conditioned leg flexion in both species). The following day we proceed to carry out the extinction part of the procedure. When our subjects arrive, however, the lab is in total darkness, the experimental room lighted only by candles. A storm has left the town without electrical power. Nevertheless, the dogs produce a normal extinction curve (or one that is inversely proportional to the difference between the present and the former illumination level). The humans do not. Believing that the laboratory, too, is without electricity, people do not produce the leg flexion at all—even to the first presentation of the tone. Moreover, responding bears no relation to the difference between the former and the present illumination level. And when the laboratory lights are restored, the dogs are largely unaffected; but the people will produce the normal extinction curve.

The dog is unaffected by the power failure not because in the dog conditioning is "cognitively impenetrable" (Pylyshyn 1980), but simply because the animal is incapable of comprehending the causal relation in question. Perhaps there are appropriate causal relations that the dog might comprehend. Or perhaps there are no causal relations the dog can *comprehend* (as opposed to show habituation for or process in some other noncognitive manner), and the dog is, like most species, incapable of cognition—a mind composed of just two components, hardwiring and learning.

Because cognition can affect conditioning so profoundly in adult humans, the presence of cognition has been advanced as necessary for conditioning to occur. For example, William Brewer (1974) and others stipulate that conditioning will occur only when the individual is aware of the relation between the CS and US. This overstates the case for cognition, I think, and creates the unnecessary impression that human conditioning is unique, dependent on prerequisites different from those of other species. Are we likely to make awareness necessary for conditioning Aplysia, for example? These overdrawn conclusions are probably the result of laboratory artifacts.

A college sophomore, when connected to a conditioning apparatus, becomes an uneasy individual who formulates and tests hypotheses, nervously conjecturing his impending fate. The hypothesis he formulates—when the instructions are truthful and the conditioning procedure is not deceitfully embedded in some other procedure—is quite likely to be correct, that is, in agreement with that of the experimenter. In this so-called unmasked or control condition, the sophomore shows conditioning (and the post-experiment interview reveals that he is aware of the CS-US relation). On the other hand, when the instructions and procedure are designed to conceal the conditioning procedure, the hypothesis he forms is likely to be incorrect, at odds with that of the experimenter. This so-called masked or experimental condition produces a rather different outcome—the sophomore typically fails to show conditioning, and the post-experiment interview reveals that he is unaware of the CS-US relation.

Does this prove that hypothesis testing and awareness of the CS-US relation are necessary for conditioning? Probably not. Rather it may prove that cognition can block conditioning and that it will, in fact, do so if the hypothesis used by the subject is sufficiently at odds with the correct one. Notice that this does not prove the converse (that correct hypotheses and awareness of the CS-US relation are themselves necessary for conditioning). Incorrect hypotheses could block conditioning, but correct hypotheses are not necessarily essential for conditioning.

Humans are conditioned in the natural world without, I suspect, either formulating hypotheses or becoming aware of the relation between the CS and US. In the natural world, conjunctions of various kinds occur—a song is heard in the presence of a friend, the scent of lilac accompanies a menacing dog, evening lights a room as one tastes a particular wine—and the individual is conditioned with neither conjecture nor hypothesis, without awareness of the CS-US relation, like any other species, indeed, like Aplysia. But in the laboratory setting, the forewarned human subject hypothesizes actively, conjecturing about procedures and instructions and their effect on his person.

The laboratory outcome is instructive for a reason different from the one normally claimed. When the individual does hypothesize, and incorrectly, conditioning can be blocked. What we see then is the power of cognition not only to override established conditioning—the power failure example—but also evidently to block the formation of new conditioning.

Which species are capable of cognition? That is, which can formulate and test hypotheses, become aware of the relation between stimuli, and comprehend the causal relation between the occurrence of one event and another? The presently considered relation between cognition and learning can serve in answering these questions. Is the species one in which learning can be affected by a system that lies outside learning? Or can learning be affected only by learning processes? These questions pose a sensitive test. To begin with, learning is acutely sensitive to cognition—judging from the human case—so that if a species were capable of cognition, the effect on learning should be readily shown. There is an additional advantage in that the test escapes all need for language: both the learning and cognition can be based on strictly perceptual information. Finally, the basic relation on which the test depends is the comprehension of causal relations. If a species cannot comprehend a relation as fundamental as this one, it is difficult to know what relation to offer as a substitute. That is, if we find the test too demanding or likely to lead to false negatives, we must find a relation (even more elementary than that of causality) whose comprehension would nonetheless qualify as a cognitive process.

On the Simulation of Hard-wiring

The "language training" studies offer an interesting and mildly ironic comment on the immensely powerful pedagogic dispositions of our species. Because humans think of themselves as primarily a learning or cognitive species, we turn to other species for examples of hard-wiring. The insect and insectlike creature is especially helpful to us in this regard because some of its hard-wired calculations actually parallel those we would perform on a cognitive basis. For instance, the spider has been shown to adjust the thickness of its strand (when spinning a web) to little weights that experimenters attach to its back. Were we faced with an analogous problem, say, parachuting while carrying different weights, obviously we could not fall back on hard-wiring but would make our adjustment with the help of a calculator (or, in an earlier epoch, slide rule).

Language is special because it turns the tables—we become the hard-wired species. Nearly all linguists and psycholinguists hold some version of this view, including those who differ radically on the particular form of the view. Learning does contribute, perhaps in the way I suggested earlier. But after the data bases are laid down, the extraction of regularities is done by hard-wiring, not learning.

The peculiar status of language—one of exceedingly few conspicuous examples of hard-wiring in the human—places a bind on a pedagogic species. We respond strangely to it, attempting to teach other species what we do not learn ourselves. Thus, we have brought long-term learning studies to bear on apes (and more recently dolphins), raising this question: Can we simulate by a process of learning that which we ourselves cannot carry out by learning? The answer has been clear for some time, but that does not mean that some of us will not go on trying.

Indeed, the number of attempts is bound to increase. Apes, dolphins, and sea lions, as of last count, will very likely become rats, pigeons, monkeys, and, I personally hope, dogs and horses (the gentler domestics) in the near future. Each case needs a specialist, devoted, knowledgeable, a defender of the species, willing to spend the four or five years required by such a project.

Such attempts will increase because the recipe for teaching "language" is now clearer. People who previously taught animals to associate one stimulus with a whole performance (for example, "press the lever for food when the light comes on") have now learned to break up the performance and to associate one stimulus with lever (rather than, say, button), another with food (rather than water), yet another with big (rather than small lever) and in that way call for the activity not with one "word" but with a combination of them.

But, let us be clear, this is not a recipe for language. It will not produce grammatical classes, hierarchical organization, recursion; nor mental representation of information by or through the would-be language system; nor any of the other properties basic to human language. But that will not deter anyone. We learn by steps—as a rule, small steps. We can therefore anticipate a future generation of animal experimentalists who will continue to teach "language" to a multiplicity of species.

3

What Is a Word?

More often than seems proper in a scientific debate, participants have lost patience and in final irritation have put the question, "Does the chimpanzee really have language?" Anything more than "yes" or "no" is seen as academic waffling. Surprisingly it is not only the media (inquiring on the phone) for whom truth is ultimately monosyllabic, but also one's colleagues. A favorite oversimplification, not of the media but of the academic, goes as follows: "Of course the ape does not have sentences, but it does have words" (Haber 1983; Danto 1983). To be sure, language can be said to consist of words and sentences, but does it follow that these elements come in only one variety, the human? The oversimplification lies in the failure to see that both words and sentences may come in many varieties.

The word may be a better target than the sentence, if only in part because it has been so profoundly neglected. Ironically, in view of the greater complexity of the sentence, we can theorize more effectively about the longer entity. As Quine noted in 1960, "What counts as a word . . . is less evident than what counts as a sentence." And things have changed little since. Linguistics is a theory of sentences not of words. (Hence the claim that the ape does not have sentences "but surely has words" does not say much.)

In this section, I will deal with some selected aspects of words. In order to get off to a running start, I will begin with an

answerable question about the difference between comprehending and producing "words." For the adult speaker comprehension and production are two aspects of one system, but
for individuals who are in the process of acquiring language
this is not the case, as we shall see. Is this peculiar to the
language-trained ape or evident also in the child?

Production versus Comprehension

We take as a given that the language of the adult speaker is a
unitary system combining production and comprehension.
Speaking and listening are simply two different aspects of the
system. There are indications, however, that this may not be
equally true for the beginning speaker. For example, Bloom
(1974) observed that the first words children produce are (often)
not the same as the first words they comprehend. A more
explicit suggestion comes from Quess and Baer (1973). In language training retarded children they found that words taught
the children in the production mode did not transfer to comprehension, and vice versa. Let us avoid any confusion by immediately making clear that the terms "production" and
"comprehension" refer to modes of use, to the child's performance as both speaker and listener respectively, not to differences in understanding. The child understands the words he
uses in both modes—those he uses in making requests (production) no less than those he responds to in requests made of
him (comprehension). This is the crux of the issue: Could the
child understand as a listener the very same words he understands as a speaker, and vice versa? Do comprehension and
production begin as separate systems?

The direct and obvious way to answer this question is to
teach separate lexicons in each mode and carry out a transfer
test, requiring the child to produce using words learned in
comprehension (and vice versa). Ethical and technical reasons
prevent us from making such a test. No creature able to produce
words spontaneously could be given such a test. Even a signing

ape would be unsuitable. The test could be given only to an individual unable to produce words but able to use words given to him by another. For example, all requests to be made of the individual might be confined to words drawn from one lexicon, while he might be taught a different lexicon for making requests of others. At some later time, when the individual was proficient in the use of both lexicons, a transfer test could follow. This is clearly a natural experiment for the chimpanzee, who cannot "make" his own plastic words but can "use" those words the experimenter gives him.

A modified version of this experiment was carried out with Peony and Elizabeth, both of whom were taught small, independent lexicons in production and comprehension. In the comprehension mode, Peony and Elizabeth were instructed to take one of several objects and in the production mode, to select the correct word (from the several words available) as a request for a particular object. For example, in tests of comprehension, the word "ball" was placed on the writing board; the animal was required to take the ball rather than any of the other objects present during the test. In tests of production, an apple and several words were present; to receive the apple, the animal had to place the word "apple" on the board. Each animal was taught ten or more words in both modes and trained until each reached a criterion of about 80 percent correct. All were then given the transfer test in which the lexicons were interchanged. Words the animal had previously placed on the board to request items from the trainer were now placed on the board by the trainer to indicate the particular object the animal should take. Conversely, words that the animal had previously only *viewed* on the board (and used to guide its choice of objects) were now given to the animal for use in requesting the object that was present. A very small difference seemingly: the word is matched to an object in one case and the object matched to a word in another.

In view of the small difference that separates production from comprehension, we were astounded to watch both animals fail trial after trial in the transfer tests from either direction. Both animals had written, say, "banana," "cantaloupe," "pear" correctly in hundreds of trials; nevertheless, when they encountered these same words on the board, they both responded at close to chance: Peony 74 errors in 177 trials and Elizabeth 120 errors in 292 trials; 58 and 59 percent correct, respectively (Premack 1976, p. 122). The failure was entirely symmetrical. When required to make requests with "ball," "keys," "clay," words they had responded to correctly in hundred of trials in the comprehension mode, they again performed nearly at chance level.

No less remarkable than this initial failure was their subsequent success. After no more than five or six exchanges of the above kind, the two systems became one. The change did not consist merely of improvement, that is, degrees of transfer from one mode to the other, but of total or perfect transfer! From that moment, any new words that were taught Peony or Elizabeth in either the comprehension or production mode transferred perfectly to the other mode. Is this peculiarity unique to the ape, or is it one that holds for all early language learners? Although we shall never directly test the child, or know the answer with certainty, Bloom's observation suggests that in the normal child as well there is an early phase in which the language the child speaks is separate from the language he hears. It is remarkable how few words the child may need to both speak and hear for the two systems to become one.

External Function of Words: Information Retrieval

At one time no property was thought to better capture the distinctive feature of language than displacement (cf. Hockett 1959). Language was glorified on grounds of displacement, celebrated for enabling the individual to talk about past or future (as well as Miami or Florence) even though sitting in Hartford. Indeed, it was principally displacement that distinguished humans from animals. The latter were stimulus bound, stuck with the reality under their noses, the "here and now."

It is a mistake, however, to give language all credit for being able to deal with times and places that differ from the present. It is not language per se but a far more basic property of mind that makes displacement possible. Any creature that can store in its mind a "representation of its world" is a potential candidate for escaping the "here and now." If the robin can store a representation of its nest in its mind, then its nest goes with it as it moves about the world. If it has stored a representation of its mate, then as it pulls an earthworm from the soil in a distant meadow, it may think of him/her. The robin does not need language in order to be reprieved from the bonds of the immediate present. To be sure, for the robin to tell another robin of the inspirational qualities of its mate's red breast, to share its mental representation with others, it would need language. And language might even help the robin think, make its representations more efficient, allow it to evoke representations of mate, nest, siblings, offspring more reliably. It is not language, however, but mental representation that makes displacement a possibility in the first place.

Are the chimpanzee's plastic words effective in retrieving the animal's mental representations? If the ape formed a mental representation of its nest (which like most birds' nests is also built in a tree) and was taught a plastic word for nest, how much of its nest could it retrieve with "nest"? The question is premature, however. We should first ask: How effective *is* ape mental representation? How preserving of information? Do ape representations retain *all* the information contained in perception or consistently lose some proportion? Do representations vary with domain? The effectiveness of the plastic words as information retrieval devices is thus a two-pronged question. First, how effective is mental representation in the ape (for one domain or the other)? And second, how much of what is stored can the ape subsequently retrieve with its plastic words?

To answer the first question, we made extensive tests on the frugivorous part of the animal's diet, using this material on grounds that if the quality of mental representation did vary with domain, apes would not slight items so dear to their heart but would picture them clearly (or as well as they could). We divided eight of the fruit in their diet into features and components: wedge, stem, peel, seed, white outlines of shape, color patches, and one nonvisual cue, taste. We then gave four animals—Sarah, Elizabeth, Peony, and Walnut, an African-born male—match-to-sample tests requiring them to match one feature of a fruit with another feature, thus to identify features that came from the same source. For instance, we gave them a taste of peach and then required them to choose between a red and a yellow patch; or showed them a white outline of an apple and then required them to choose between the stem of an apple and of a pear; or presented a peach pit and required them to choose between a peel of peach and of banana, etc. There were about twenty-four tests of this general kind, the logic for all of which was the same: the more you know about an item, the less you should require to identify it. By analogy, if pictures of your family were cut into pieces, you could prove your good mental representation of your family by your ability to match different pieces of the same individual (the little finger of your spouse with his/her ear, eye, nose, hair, etc.).

All apes tested performed well, though Sarah's results were especially impressive; she could use every cue correctly. The other three animals, although generally accurate, were more successful with some parts than with others.

As for them, it was possible to rank-order the informativeness of the several cues. Not surprisingly, the whole fruit was the most informative (i.e., more parts could be matched to it than to anything else).

But color and peel were almost as effective; the chimpanzees were almost as able to match the seed, stem, shape, and wedge to a patch of color as to the whole fruit itself. Taste was less informative, followed by a tie between shape, wedge and stem. Trailing all the components was seed, the least informative cue of all. Differences of this kind do not change the main finding. Chimpanzees, Sarah especially, but the other animals as well, can store detailed representations of items such as fruit (Premack and Premack 1983).

The chimpanzee, therefore, should be able to think about things that are not present. It could do this most effectively, of course, if its thoughts of, say, fruit did not flit sporadically through its mind but could be evoked reliably by the names of the fruit. There were already suggestions that the plastic words could serve the animal in this manner. One suggestion came from an extremely early stage of language training with Sarah; from the beginning she was able to use the plastic words to request preferred fruits that were *not* present (Premack 1971). In another case, she was successfully taught the word "brown" through the instruction "brown color of chocolate" given to her at a time when no chocolate (or any other brown object) was present (Premack 1976, p. 202). Cases of this kind already suggest that the plastic words could invoke mental representations, enabling the animal to think of fruit that were not at hand.

We obtained additional evidence of a more formal kind by repeating the memory series above, but with the parts of the fruit replaced by the plastic names of the fruit as the alternatives. The animal was given, for instance, a taste of peach as the sample, which was followed by the plastic words for "peach" and "apple" as alternatives, or given a white outline of banana followed by the plastic words for "banana" and "orange," or a patch of yellow followed by the plastic words for "lemon" and "grape."

How effective were the plastic words? We can answer by comparing the animal's success when the alternatives consisted of words in one case and of physical features in another. Although this comparison was not instructive with Sarah (because she was completely successful with both the words and physical features), it was informative with the other three animals. Since they were more successful with some features than with others, we could rank-order the effectiveness of the physical parts of the fruit for them. For example, color was the most effective physical cue for all three animals: they made fewer errors when the alternatives consisted of colors than of any other part of the fruit. Yet they made still fewer errors when the alternatives consisted of the names of the fruit. The plastic words served these animals better than did any physical part of the fruit. In fact, all three animals were about as effective in matching parts of the fruit to the names of the fruit as they were in matching the same parts to the whole fruits. This outcome suggests answers to both of our original questions. First, apparently the information in the ape's mental representation (of fruit at least) preserves the information in its perception, or the apes would have done better with the whole fruit than with the names. Second, the plastic words are extremely effective devices for retrieving information.

What is Stored in the Ape's Mind?

Words in the human case do not serve only to retrieve information; they are presumably a part of the information that is stored. Can we make the same claim for the ape? Do the words (and sentences) taught the ape leave the writing board and make their way into the ape's mind, so that part of the information that is stored there consists of the language that the ape has been taught? Although this key question is a tricky one—the relation between mental events and behavior is seldom simple and direct—it is only hard, not hopeless.

In a classic approach to this problem, we ask whether an individual's performance on certain tasks is facilitated by teaching him names for the items that are to be used in the task. For instance, can the child identify an object better (following a short delay) if he has been taught a name for the object? There is the suggestion that he can (Spiker 1956), but what does such an effect prove? Suppose we could duplicate the effect in the chimpanzee; would this establish that the plastic words had become a part of the information stored in the chimpanzee's mind?

I think not, for the effect, which is one of short-term memory, adds little to what is already shown by the use of the word as an information retrieval device. In large part, the test requires the individual to do the opposite of what was required in the first test, that is, to retrieve the name of the object by using perception or representation of the object (rather than the converse, using words to retrieve representations). The whole process may go as follows: when shown an object that has been named, the individual thinks of its name and then rehearses with the name during the delay interval. The advantage to the child may come simply from the vocal nature of the word: the vocal event may be more subject to voluntary control than the visual image of the object. If so, we could not expect to see a comparable advantage in the chimpanzee since both its words and objects are visual.

Perhaps the ape has a preferred form of representation: when shown objects, it may convert them into words (or when shown words convert them into objects), finding the storage of one kind of item easier than the other. Alternatively, even if the ape has no natural asymmetry of this kind, we may be able to induce one by requiring the animal to discriminate among highly similar objects (whose names, however, are highly dissimilar) or, conversely, highly dissimilar objects (whose names are highly similar). In such a case, whether presented with names or with objects, the animal may store that set whose members are the more discriminable. These are, for the moment, unanswered questions, though the test designs that could answer them are easily described. In this case, we are separated from answers by nothing more than the usual tedious experiments.

Does learning language change the way in which the ape is able to think? Language training *does* appear to confer a general advantage, enabling the animal to solve more abstract problems than it otherwise might. For instance, while all apes can match, say, half an apple to half an apple, only the language-trained ape matches half an apple to half a cylinder of water (Woodruff and Premack 1981). Similarly, while all apes match X to X (rather than Y), only the language-trained ape matches XX to YY (rather than PQ) and PQ to XY (rather than LL) (Premack 1983). Thus language training appears to enable the ape to go beyond physical similarity and to compute equivalences on more conceptual grounds. But this is a suggestion based on a serendipitous comparison; we await the outcome of an experiment in progress—comparing equated groups of language- and non-language-trained apes—before drawing firm conclusions (Premack 1983).

Returning to our original question: Does teaching the ape language change either the form or content of its mental representation? To answer this elusive question, we gave both children and language-trained apes special match-to-sample tests in which the natural features of objects were either distorted or concealed. The subjects' success in recognizing these camouflaged objects was to serve as the basis for inferring how the objects were mentally represented.

In one test we concealed the color of fruit by painting them white and then gave match-to-sample tests in which the sample consisted of a patch of color and the alternatives of two of the fruit (for instance, a red patch as sample, a white apple and a white banana as alternatives). Three language-trained apes tested in this way performed well above chance, at about the 80 percent level (Premack 1976, p. 307). In the next step, we changed the white paint to blue and repeated the tests (so that now both the apple and banana were blue); the average accuracy fell to only about 65 percent. In the third and last step, we used two nonveridical colors, making one of the two fruit blue and the other orange; accuracy fell to chance in all three animals (Premack, unpublished data).

Why should the apes succeed when the fruit are white, do less well when they are blue, and fail altogether when they are of two different colors? The answer could lie in the animal's representation of the fruit. Suppose the ape's mental representation of the fruit is strictly imaginal and has no discursive component. This could impose limits on its use, limits compatible with the possibility that the animal can "imagine" the color of the painted fruit while at the same time *perceiving* white but cannot "imagine" the color of the painted fruit while perceiving two different colors. Indeed, perceiving a color other than white strains the system.

The hypothesis that perception (of a certain kind) can interfere with the imagining or picturing of an item, while on the right track, is in its present form too simple. It is not the *number* of other colors perceived that interferes with the imagining of an object of a different color. Even the ape can imagine one color while perceiving at least two others. We have already encountered a case (in the previous section on information retrieval) in which the perception of two colors did not in the least interfere with the animal's correct selection of a third color. It is a case in which the sample consisted of a patch of color, and the alternatives consisted of the *names* of the fruit, not the painted fruit. The names of fruit have both form and color: the name for apple is (triangular) blue, that for banana (square) pink, etc. Yet the animals had no difficulty matching, say, the (blue) word for apple to a red patch. All four animals—Sarah, Peony, Elizabeth, and even Walnut, who was taught only a few words— performed remarkably well: 4 errors in 52 trials summed over the animals (Premack 1976, pp. 306–307). Nevertheless, they had great difficulty matching an actual apple (painted blue) to the red patch. Although the blue word serves nicely in the recall of the (red) apple, the painted blue apple does not. Either the blue apple is not recognized as an apple (highly unlikely) or perceiving a blue apple interferes with the imagining of a red one, a sharp contrast with the blue word, which produces no such interference with imagining.

The adverse effect of perception on imagining may also hold for words when considered as objects rather than names. For instance, perceiving a distorted word (orange triangle or green square) could interfere with the imagining of the normal word (blue triangle or pink square). We can test this assumption as follows: make the sample a blue patch (the normal color of the word apple) and the alternatives the words apple and banana. Make the former orange rather than blue in color, the latter green instead of pink. The test requires the animal to match blue, the normal color of the word apple, with the triangle now painted orange, that is, to imagine the blue triangle (name of apple) while perceiving a (distorted) orange triangle. This could be as costly as, say, imagining a red apple while perceiving a blue one and should impair performance.

Contrast this case with one in which the sample is a red patch and the alternatives remain the same ("apple" and "banana" painted orange and green, respectively). The animal must now match red, a property of the referent, with the distorted word for apple. In the former test, the animal was required to match a property of the normal word with a distorted word; in the present test, to match a property of the referent with a distorted word. Only the first test requires the imagining of the normal word while perceiving the distorted one; therefore only the first test should be costly, leading to impaired performance. In the second test, the animals could recognize the word on the basis of shape and size alone (ignoring color altogether), circumventing the need to imagine anything at all.

While they can look at a blue word and "see" a red apple, they apparently cannot look at a blue apple and "see" a red one (or the cost of the latter is far greater than that of the former). The imagining of a normal object will be impaired by the perception of a distorted version of the object; but the perception of an object's name—even though differing at least as much from the object as the distorted version of the object— does not interfere with imagining the object.

What are the boundary conditions of the impairment effect? The only apparent impairment we have encountered so far involves the same object (for instance, the effect of a distorted apple on imagining a real one). We have speculated that comparable results can be found for words. Should we conclude, therefore, that impairment is a narrow phenomenon, restricted to the case in which it is the same item that is both perceived and imagined? And why do objects and their names escape the impairment? Is it simply because words and objects are physically very different or, more interestingly, because they belong to different categories and are processed independently? It remains to be seen whether impairment is a narrow phenomenon, restricted to sameness of item, or a broader one in which even the perception of one object, say, lion, interferes with the imagining of another object, say, tiger (or analogously, the perception of one word, "lion," interferes with the imagining of another word, "tiger").

When free from perceptual interference, the chimpanzee is evidently capable of imagining items accurately and of using images effectively. These capacities were demonstrated by match-to-sample tests which presented the animals with alternatives that consisted of fruit painted white (white being a non-impairing condition) and samples that were the names of colors. For instance, in one test the alternatives were a lemon and a cherry, both painted white; the sample was the name "yellow." The plastic color names are colorless — different shades of grey that vary in shape and size. The animal was required to picture or imagine the color of the lemon as well as the color associated with the small, grey plastic word that named yellow and to match these two internal representations. (Note that when the white (painted) lemon was matched to the name "yellow," the color yellow was not present.) The test posed no problem for any of the three animals tested — Sarah, Peony, Elizabeth. With white fruit as alternatives, they performed equally well whether the sample consisted of an actual patch of color or the name of the color (Premack 1976, p. 307).

The impairment effect we appear to have found offers a tool for comparing mental representations of different species (or children at different developmental stages). One species may be much more sensitive to the impairment effect than another — but not necessarily because perception impairs imagining in the one species more than in another. On the contrary, even if the impairment effect per se were equal for two species, the cost of the impairment might be far greater for the one species than for the other. The nature of the mental representation should determine the cost. For a species whose internal representation was primarily imaginal, the inability to imagine accurately could be disastrous; whereas for a species whose representation was primarily discursive, impaired imagery might have a negligible effect.

If this view is correct, human performance on the distorted fruit tests administered to the chimpanzees should have a markedly different outcome. Since human representation is both imaginal and discursive, humans need not resort to imagining one color while perceiving others; they can also take advantage of words and phrases. For example, they can represent the natural color of the blue apple as "red" and match this with "apple is a small red fruit," part of their discursive representation of apple. To test this interpretation, we examined both a younger and an older group of children in much the same way as we had the chimpanzees.

In testing the children, we were obliged to abandon the use of fruit because pilot studies showed that for the children fruit did not have the simple invariant relation with color; for the apes apples in the laboratory were always red (but in the experience of the children apples were also yellow and green). Three characters from *Sesame Street* plus Santa Claus provided four dolls that overcame this problem; the dolls were as invariant in color for the children as was the fruit for the chimpanzees. We painted all the dolls white for the first test, all pink for the second, and half of them pink, half orange for the third (the changes in color were necessitated by the natural colors of the items). The children were tested as the apes had been, a patch of color (2 × 4 inch card) serving as the sample and two of the painted dolls as alternatives. The four dolls were paired in all possible ways, and three trials were given on each pair. The left/right order and pairs were counterbalanced as much as possible over the twelve trials in the session.

Ten children, average age four years and six months, were given three sessions, first on the white, next on the pink, and then on the pink and orange dolls. Seven of the ten children passed the white series (eleven of twelve correct or better), and of these seven only one failed any other series; he failed both the one-color and two-color series. Thus, with the exception of one child, the variations that had disrupted the apes, the change from white to color and, even more, to two colors, had no effect on the children. Either the children passed the tests completely or they did not pass them at all.

We gave the identical tests to eight younger children, average age three years and one month. All eight children failed all of the tests, the series based on the white dolls no less than those based on the colored ones. Did these younger children fail because, having less familiarity with Santa Claus and the *Sesame Street* characters, they had poorly formed mental representations of the dolls or because they could not recognize the normal doll even in its white version (let alone its colored one)? After the tests were completed, we sought to answer these questions by interviewing the children. First, we asked them to name the white dolls, which they were all able to do, and then we asked them to identify their normal colors. Each child was given one white doll at a time and asked to name its color; only one child was successful in naming all four colors correctly. Recognition tests, given next, did not help matters. When told the name of the color of one of the two white dolls, the children still could not point to the appropriate doll. Their failure was either complete—four of the eight children scored zero—or close to it.

Thus the children performed quite differently from the apes. Either the children could not do the task at all—true for all younger children and for 30 percent of older ones—or with one exception they performed perfectly on the whole series. The children's performance (unlike the apes') did not suffer when a nonwhite color was introduced or deteriorate further when two such colors were introduced. Why, however, did the apes succeed with the white fruit when the younger children failed altogether, even with the white dolls? (Although the children could name the white dolls, they could not recall or even recognize the names of their colors.) Perhaps this is simply because color is not the basic identifying feature for the dolls that it appears to be for the fruit. To clarify the comparison between the ape and the children, we shall have to find a common set of items that can be used with both species.

We prepared another test exactly like the previous one but replaced color with shape. Since color is in some respects a unique feature, we wondered about the generality of our results: would they hold for other features? One peculiarity of color is that the normal color of an object cannot simply be hidden; it can only be changed. For instance, in order to mask the color of an apple, one can only paint the apple white or some other color. This restriction does not apply to shape. The shape of an apple can be masked in two ways: by changing its shape by, for instance, building a square apple (analogous to painting the apple blue) or placing the apple in a box with a porthole. The appropriate porthole gives a clear view of part of the apple while at the same time obscuring its shape.

We used four fruit—apple, banana, pear, and orange—and presented the fruit in identical small white boxes (2 × 3.5 × 2.5 inches), each with a small porthole on the top. As before, test trials consisted of a sample and two alternatives, but now the sample was the shape (cut from white paper) of one of the fruit, and the alternatives were two fruit, each contained in a white box with a porthole on the top. Conceivably, a child's ability to remember the shape of the fruit could be influenced by the shape of the porthole through which he/she viewed the fruit. To test this possibility, all the portholes in the first test series were made the same shape (round), while in the second series they were of two shapes (square and triangular). The four boxed fruits were paired in all possible ways, and three trials were given on each pair. The left/right order and pairs were counterbalanced as much as possible over the twelve trials of each series.

All ten of the older children passed both series, while only three of the younger children did. The shape of the portholes had no effect; in fact, both groups did slightly better on the two-porthole than on the one-porthole series, suggesting that practice was beneficial. One might suppose that a child who passed the shape test would be helped to pass the color one, the paradigm of the two tests being exactly the same. But there was no hint of this. Of the three younger children who passed the shape test, two happened to be in the subgroup receiving the color test after the shape test; they failed the color test like the rest of the younger children.

Perhaps the test is more difficult with color because it is more difficult to recall an underlying feature when that feature has been "distorted" rather than merely concealed, as is the case with shape. We cannot use the present results to make a decision, but need to contrast "distortion" with "concealment" using the same feature, such as *square apple* versus *apple viewed through a porthole*.

The non-language-trained ape may, when tested, perform less well than the language-trained ape. It may respond like the young child, failing when the alternatives are differently colored as well as when they are similarly colored or even white. If language-trained animals are more competent with this test series than the non-language-trained, we would consider that the animal's mental representation was enhanced by language learning. The performance of the language-trained animal, relative to that of the older child, does not portray any such benefit. Quite the contrary, the child-ape comparison suggests that, whether or not the ape has a deficiency in discursive representation, its acquisition of an artificial language does not correct the deficiency. Apparently, the language does not enter the ape's mind, providing it with a representational system that permits it to perform these tests at the level of the older child. When examined alongside certain of the apes' successes, the failure would provide additional interest.

Despite failing the representational tests, the apes nonetheless succeed in producing or judging descriptions. They succeed in judging the correspondence between a condition and a discursive (plastic word) representation of the condition, which indicates that the ape can use *external* discursive representations whether written by the ape or by others. It can, for example, place plastic word "sentences" into correspondence with the conditions these "sentences" describe. But the ape cannot "write 'sentences' inside its own head"—cannot spontaneously produce discursive representations internally.

Such a combination of results makes it irresistible to attempt teaching the ape to write discursive (plastic word) representations of the "distorted objects," circumventing entirely the need to rely on pictorial representation. For instance, in offering the ape a violet apple and a blue banana as alternatives, and a red patch as the sample, we teach the ape to place the plastic names "apple" and "banana" beside the distorted fruit before making a choice. When trained in this fashion, if the ape could pass tests it would otherwise fail, we would have additional evidence that the ape can do *outside* its head what it cannot do *inside*.

On Not Confusing Word Use with Word Meaning

We should not confuse the *use* of words (which concern general cognitive factors) with the specific properties of words (mental representation and retrieval of information) that we have identified here. One example of this kind of confusion is demonstrated in a study by the Rumbaughs (1978). Four young chimpanzees being trained to operate a keyboard connected to automatic food dispensers persisted in operating the key producing chocolate candy long after the candy dispenser was empty. The Rumbaughs concluded that this was proof that the keys were not "real words" ("decontextualized symbols") for the animals but merely "ritualistically associated motor patterns" (ibid., p. 266). People, the Rumbaughs assure us, would not persist in operating the key for candy once the dispenser was empty. They would shift instead to the operation of a key yielding a less preferred item (thus demonstrating possession of "real words").

Perhaps the only valid conclusion to be drawn from the Rumbaughs' study has nothing to do with "real words" or "motor patterns" but concerns a far simpler point: the chimpanzees did not form a causal connection between the operation of the dispenser and the pressing of the key. In time, the animals did stop pressing only the key for candy and shifted to alternate keys, but there is no evidence that the shift resulted from a recognition that the dispenser was empty. Pigeons too will learn to stop pressing the same key after repeated failure and shift to other keys. The claim that either pigeons or three-year-old apes do so because they have developed an understanding of the causal relations between keys and dispensers is ill founded.

Suppose for the sake of argument that both apes and pigeons did learn the causal relations between the key and the dispenser. Would such an insight result in establishing the key as a word? Can we also say that the child who says "cookie" is not using a "real word" unless he understands the causal relation between saying "cookie" and being given a cookie (by mother)? Roughly speaking, in order to gloss the child's "cookie," we require that the child say "cookie" when he wants a cookie, not some other item. The child is not required to understand the causal relations involved in the effective vocalization of "cookie."

To be sure, we wish to know whether the child who wants a cookie says "cookie" only when mother is present or says "cookie" when mother is absent as well and whether the child entertains different hopes and expectations on each occasion. This informs us of the child's grasp of the effective use of words in the appropriate context. Comprehension of this kind is a well-known form of metacognition, developing rather slowly in the child (Flavell 1978).

The ability to grasp the conditions of effective use of words (i.e., communication) must be distinguished from that of grasping the conditions that warrant glossing a response as a "word." There is no benefit in confusing the two. A recent study with our four young chimpanzees, who were then in an early stage of learning plastic words, helped preserve the distinction. In training the animals, we placed objects around the test room and showed the animal the plastic name for each object, one at a time. We then required each animal to find and return (to the trainer) the object whose plastic name was presented. After about three hundred trials, all four animals were reasonably proficient at this task. We then introduced some probes. The trainer, instead of holding the language board (on which the plastic word adhered) directly before her, making the word conspicuous to the animal, tilted the board to one side, which reduced the word's visibility, and sometimes even turned the board completely around, rendering the word totally invisible.

Three of the four animals went immediately to the concealed word and twisted their bodies so as to achieve a better view of the word. Two of them grasped the inverted board (pulling it away from the trainer's chest) and brought the word into view. In marked contrast, the fourth animal did nothing about the concealed word; she neither adjusted her posture nor touched the board. On probe trials the animal performed at chance level, but on regular trials she performed well. In fact, her 88 percent correct on regular trials compared favorably with the others, putting her in a tie for first place.

Can we say that three animals had true symbols while the fourth had a "ritualistically conditioned motor pattern"? Rather than reflecting differences in the symbolic status of the words, the results yield something comparable to what we may learn from talking to children in a noisy room. Does the child draw closer to the speaker in order to hear? Does the child raise his own voice so that he may be heard? Does he look into his listener's face? If certain expressions fail to appear on the face of the listener, does the child repeat himself until he sees appropriate expressions? Or does he speak with total disregard for conditions around him (thus resembling the young ape who, having taken no steps to restore the visibility of the word, goes off blindly to find an object whose name she cannot possibly know)?

The metacognitive grasp of the conditions on which communication depends, on the one hand, and the use of items to be regarded as words, on the other, need not be conflated. They are not difficult to separate. Indeed, they are sufficiently separable to incline us to inquire how these competences affect one another, whether the development of one depends on the other. It seems that the relation between semantics and pragmatics can be profitably studied in this straightforward situation.

Teaching Words Nonostensively

Virtually all the words that have been taught to animals have been taught ostensively, that is, by pointing to the referent and directly associating it with the word. For example, a piece of apple is placed before the animal along with a blue triangular piece of plastic; when the animal uses the plastic appropriately, placing it on the writing board, it is given the apple. Even later, after "name of" has been taught and words can be elegantly introduced with the instruction "X (an unused piece of plastic) name of Y (a familiar but not yet named object)," we do not escape ostension; the object Y is present along with X, the name to be. Animals have been taught very few words that do not depend on pointing to the item that is to be named.

A principal exception is based on the use of the predicates "color of," "shape of," and the like. They can be used to generate new instances of themselves, in a manner that is nonostensive. For example, we taught Sarah the word "brown" with the instruction "brown color of chocolate" ("chocolate" and "color of" being known to her, of course), given at a time when no chocolate (or any other brown object) was present. When subsequently told "take brown," she correctly selected the brown object from the set of four colored objects present. Although, unfortunately, this is our only example of this kind, there is no reason to doubt that apes could be taught any number of words nonostensively with the predicates in question. However, the productive use of these predicates is not especially instructive: it merely confirms what we already know from other sources. The animal can retrieve its mental representations with arbitrary items that have been associated with the representations.

Two other nonostensive procedures are explicit definition and definition by description. We attempted to introduce an approximation of one of the logical connectives, the exclusive "or," by explicit definition, relying upon the connectives "and," "if-then" plus the negative particle "no" that had already been introduced. The attempt was unsuccessful, though perhaps only for technical reasons (Premack 1976, pp. 244–49). The information contained in the definition was not motivationally compelling but artificial and rather like that of a nursery rhyme. "If you take banana don't take apple, and if you take apple don't take banana same take banana or apple" (in brief, don't take both of them). What we needed instead was a circumstance which, when combined with the information in the definition, would have conveyed the message: "You are the star performer here and therefore can have first choice between these two highly desirable toys. But you can't have both of them; you can have one or the other." To be effective, the explicit definition must be not only formally complete but also motivationally apt. The definition we used is more likely to have worked with a computer or college sophomore than with an ape.

We did not try introducing words by providing *descriptions* of the item to be named rather than the item itself—regrettably, since this procedure is appreciably less demanding than explicit definition and more likely to have been successful. For example, cantaloupe might have been introduced as "rough skin round fruit," since the two kinds of words needed, properties and categories, are ones that Sarah learned (Premack 1976, pp. 177, 214).

There is an important class of words that could not be introduced either by ostension or by any of the three nonostensive procedures we considered. The word "idea" is a good example of this class. There is, of course, no hope of describing ideas, and any attempt at a dictionary-type definition would fail (with a child no less than with an ape). There is really only one way to teach such words—through examples provided in the course of conversation. "John has good ideas, Mary poor ones, Bill lots of them. . . . Where did you get that idea? I don't think your mother will like that idea." Sentences of this kind, though referring to quite arcane aspects of the persons and conditions in question, will nonetheless enable the child to form an idea of "idea." I do not pretend to know how the child does this. It is certainly mysterious, especially when one considers the nonspecificity of the information provided by the examples. Ideas are properties of persons and are subject to variation in number and quality. That is virtually all that is clear from the examples; this combination of properties is certain to apply to legions of items. Nevertheless, the examples work, for in time the child's own use of "idea," his examples, will enable the adult to assess the child's progress and to adjust his next round of examples, in an effort to correct any misapprehensions the child's examples may reveal, thus bringing the child closer to adult usage.

Does it really work that way, by a converging set of examples, or is explicit correction needed at some point? Is the process one that is measured in weeks, months, or years? Are the child's first examples simply copies of the adult's examples? Are his first original uses wide of the mark? Through how many corrections does a word of this kind pass before arriving at the adult usage? Is the path of semantic progress smooth or jagged? Finally, what proportion of the human lexicon is acquired in this way? The literature is silent on these basic issues. Of one issue, however, we can be reasonably certain: no animal is likely to acquire any part of its lexicon in this manner.

The Importance of Negative Exemplars

Our first objective in attempting to teach language to the ape is to find the pieces into which it divides the world. We have no occasion sentences to go on, so must take a different approach. Suppose we wish to teach the animal a name for apple. We must first determine if the animal can discriminate apples from nonapples, using either a sorting or match-to-sample procedure. We give the animal various positive and negative exemplars of apple and require it to separate them. What we use as positive exemplars will depend on our aspirations for the word *apple*. Do we want "apple" to apply to everything we accept by that name? If so, we must include all varieties of apples, in all stages of growth and decay, and the like. The more important consideration is what to use as negative exemplars. Although, regrettably, there are no mechanical procedures for generating negative exemplars, their choice is of the utmost importance, for the interpretation we can defend for the animal's success with the positive exemplars hinges on the negative exemplars.

Suppose, for example, that our negative exemplars consist of nuts, bolts, handcombs, and pencils. The animal's success in creating two piles, one of apples and the other of the items mentioned, would hardly warrant the claim that the positive pile represents apples. Obviously, the "apple" pile may represent not apples but edibles, natural items, or even just colored things. There is too much semantic space between our negative and positive exemplars. We can reduce the space as follows. Consider all the classes into which apple could possibly be sorted and pick the one that is most proximal. Edible is more proximal than natural item, fruit more proximal than edible. Without inventing classes tailored for the occasion, such as "fruit of the northern plains," "fruit into which the beak of a crow penetrates from three to five centimeters," and so on, fruit may be as proximal as we can get. If so, we must then select our negative exemplars from this class. In lieu of a mechanical procedure for generating negative exemplars, we can use a rule of thumb: draw negative exemplars from the most proximal class. This will not eliminate all possible errors, but it will protect against some of the worst.

The animal's ability to separate positive and negative exemplars establishes that it can draw the distinction in question, and thus we should be able to teach it a name for the distinction. The converse does not hold, however. The animal's inability to separate the exemplars (as we would separate them) does not establish that it is incapable of drawing the distinction in question. It is a common finding that young children can neither sort certain exemplars by themselves nor follow the adult sorting of them: but when told what the distinction is, they can then sort new exemplars of the distinction as accurately as an adult. One example of this kind, noted by Kim Dolgin (1981) in her thesis research, is the distinction between intentional and unintentional acts. Three-and-a-half-year-old children cannot follow the adult sorting of brief videotapes depicting intentional and unintentional acts. But after a discussion of fewer than ten words concerning "on purpose," they then sort novel videotapes as accurately as college sophomores. Another striking example concerns the semantic concepts of agent, recipient, and instrument of the action, which I will discuss at length in a later section. The four-year-old child is already in considerable advance of the three-and-a-half-year-old. By age four, though puzzling discrepancies still appear, the child approaches adult performance: a near equivalence between the distinctions that can be drawn on verbal and nonverbal grounds.

The ape, I suspect, is in the same boat as the three-and-a-half-year-old child. Sarah, for example, could not follow our sorting of the videotapes depicting intentional and unintentional acts, yet from tests of another kind, we have reason to believe that this is a distinction she can draw (Premack and Woodruff 1981). We cannot assist the ape as we can the child. Sharing no language with the ape, sharing nothing but the concepts we may possibly have in common, we can do little more than place before the ape would-be exemplars of these concepts. Either the exemplars succeed or our communication with the ape is at an end. We can always try other exemplars, hoping they will be more evocative. But I have never succeeded with an ape on a second try. One tends somehow to pick the best exemplars on the first try.

Teaching a name for a distinction is commonly thought to modify the distinction, to increase its salience and above all its abstractness. This view appears prominently in the animal language work where, as evidence for the abstractness part of the claim, we are told about the remarkable extensions animals make when applying the words they have been taught. Suppose an animal is taught "open" using the opening of a door as the exemplar and is then found to apply "open" to the opening of a drawer, a book, even a mouth. The report of these extensions will be accompanied by a rush of excitement, the underlying implication of which is clear: the extensions are undeniable evidence of language, for where but in language do we find abstractness of this kind?

In fact, we have no evidence that the extension shown by the animal (in applying words to exemplars beyond those used in training) is in any way affected by its having been taught the words. The same degree of abstractness may be shown by the animal in nonverbal sorting tasks carried out before the animal was taught any words. Words should, of course, reflect whatever abstractness may have been present beforehand, but it is not clear why they should add to the abstractness.

Indeed, the teaching of words may even impair or interfere with abstractness. The impairment may be only temporary, though even as such it would show that abstractness predated the language training and could not have been introduced by it. Suppose, for example, that in our sorting task for apple we find the animal has a concept of apple roughly as abstract as our own: it successfully collected together all possible varieties, shapes, and parts of apples. In teaching it a word for apple, however, we could not use all possible exemplars; for convenience we used mainly red winesaps. What effect will this have on the animal's use of the word "apple"? In all likelihood the animal will surmount the restricted exemplars of its training and apply the word broadly, as broadly (though not more broadly than) predicted by the preverbal sorting.

If we record the latency of the animal's judgment, we are likely to find that it says "apple" most quickly when the exemplar is a red winesap, less quickly when a red jonathan, more slowly for a red delicious, and slowest of all for the green and yellow varieties. Even if the animal should use the word quite correctly, in keeping with the preverbal sorting, the latency data testify that the word is not the source of the abstractness. On the contrary, the preverbal concept is the source of the abstractness. The word must inevitably contaminate that abstractness, for the word cannot be associated with all possible exemplars— only with specific ones.

Consider another example of the same kind in which an animal is taught names for numbers. Apes are capable of matching numbers of up to about five (five versus four may be their limit; they tend to fail on five versus six; see Hayes and Nissen 1971; Woodruff and Premack 1981). Suppose in teaching the names for the numbers we equate the areas of all the sets used as exemplars except that for 3; here we make the total area covered by the items in the set several times larger than that for any other set. Or in another approach, we use uncolored items to exemplify the sets for 1, 2, 4, and 5, but bright red items to exemplify the set for 3. Both of these approaches would show, I suspect, that the abstractness of "three" would be compromised.

The animal should be more likely to err in the use of "three" than in the use of names of the other numbers. These errors should show up in tests as simple as those of match to sample. For example, if we give the animal four bananas as the sample and the words "three" and "four" as alternatives, it should correctly choose "four." But if we change the sample to four bright red apples, the animal might now err, incorrectly choosing "three." Even if the animal does not succumb to its personal experience, to the idiosyncracies of a history in which "three" is always red while the other numbers are uncolored, even if it resists these influences and chooses correctly, the animal may still choose "four" more slowly when the sample consists of four apples than of four bananas.

The animal's *concept* of three may be unaffected by the biased training; if we exemplify three with actual items, the animal may use this nonverbal sample as accurately as it uses nonverbal samples of the other numbers. But we need only substitute the word "three" for the nonverbal sample to reveal that "three" is not as neutral a representation of 3 as the other words are representations of their numbers. It is not clear how words can generate abstractness; what is clear is how they can contaminate it.

The role of negative exemplars, which we have seen to be critical in sorting tasks, is no less critical in assigning glosses to the words we teach the animal. Suppose we have taught the ape a word for the relation between a color and an object instantiating that color: "color of," as in "red color of apple." The animal passes the standard transfer tests, answering questions about novel cases. For instance, when asked "What is the color of grass?" ("? color of grass"), it answers "green"; when asked "What is the relation between yellow and lemon?" ("Yellow ? lemon"), it answers "color of"; and when asked "What is blue the color of?" ("blue color of ?"), it answers "grapes."

The weight we assign these answers must vary with the alternatives among which the animal chooses when giving its answers. For instance, if the animal answers "green color of grass," choosing "green" rather than "shoe, run, dog, Jack," no weight can be assigned to its answer; in any case, far less than if the alternatives were "red, orange, big, round." Similarly, if, when answering that the relation between yellow and lemon is "color of," the alternatives were "shape of, size of, texture of, name of," we can be suitably impressed; not so if they were "goat, car, watermelon, swim." The gloss we assign to a word is defended by the words the animal does *not* choose, and these count only if they stand in the closest possible semantic relation to the correct word.

Unfortunately, not all words have obvious semantic neighbors. The set consisting of "shape of," "color of," "size of," "texture of" is nearly ideal. Intuitively, each member of the set is admirably close to the other; we can think of no alternatives to slip between them. What, for instance, could we wedge between "color of" and "shape of"? Of course, if we could think of such a word, we would have to include it among the alternatives given the animal. Should the animal succeed despite this even finer division of semantic space, the confidence we had in our glosses would be increased. Notice that the close semantic contrasts with which we seek to challenge the animal are not necessarily for the animal's benefit. In fact, the animal may assign exactly the same extension to "size of," "color of," and the like whether we challenge it or not. The didactic value of the challenges are more for the teacher's benefit than the student's. They test the student, advising the teacher whether or not he has been successful.

Not all words are best contrasted with other words. For instance, "name of," the relation between a name and the object named, seems better contrasted with objects than with other words. Typically, I included "name of" in the set containing "color of" and "shape of," though reluctantly, for it is obviously a deviant member of that set. But there is no other set I could find for which "name of" is not a deviant member. I considered "name of" to be better evaluated by giving the animal instructions contrasting, say, "insert apple in dish" with "insert name of apple in dish," offering as alternatives both pieces of apple and the name for apple, as well as other names. When given 17 instructions of the general kind, Sarah was correct on 14 of them ($p < .05$) (Premack 1976, p. 167).

"Gavagai" and Plastic Words

The problems we face in attempting to teach language to a nonhuman species bear a considerable resemblance to those facing Quine's linguist (1960), who attempts to translate a language radically different from his own. The linguist, hearing the native utter "gavagai," assumes that the sound is a word and undertakes to figure out what caused the native to say "gavagai." Basically, he proceeds by varying the "stimulation" while he says "gavagai" and then recording the native's assent or dissent. Suppose the linguist's tests disclose that the native assents to rabbit, while at the same time dissenting to small dogs, white cats, and jumping frogs. The linguist tentatively adopts the hypothesis that rabbit is critical but (while proceeding with the translation of other words) keeps watching for additional evidence that will confirm his hypothesis against still other alternatives. The linguist cannot possibly stop to design all the tests that are needed for certainty; he is unlikely to get beyond the first word. Rather than try for certainty on the first round, he will remain on the alert for a number of factors in the course of this continuing work. For example, he will be relieved to find that long-eared deer, jumping kangaroos, and soft-furred minks do not occasion "gavagai"; nor do chickens or ducks, which, like rabbits, are eaten by the native. Absolute certainty as to the stimulus meaning of "gavagai" may be far off, but it will be moved closer by these and other discoveries.

Quine draws a major distinction between what he calls "stimulus meaning" and the "meaning of terms." The stimulus meaning of "gavagai" is simply the stimulus or condition that prompts the native's assent to the linguist's "gavagai"—presumably, the appearance of a rabbit. But we cannot take the stimulus meaning of "gavagai" to establish the meaning of the "term rabbit" (or even to guarantee that "gavagai" and "rabbit" are coextensive terms, true of the same things). For as Quine observed: "Who knows but what the objects to which this term applies are not rabbits after all, but mere stages, or brief temporal segments, of rabbits? . . . Or perhaps the objects to which 'gavagai' applies are all and sundry undetached parts of rabbits." Or if that is not trouble enough, consider a third alternative— "gavagai" might name the fusion of all rabbits, "that single though discontinuous portion of the spatiotemporal world that consists of rabbits" (p. 52), an alternative Quine adopts from Nelson Goodman (1951).

Quine asks whether the inability to decide among these interpretations is due to a special fault in his formulation of stimulus meaning or whether a little additional pointing and questioning might not resolve the indecision. Additional pointing would not help, he decides:

Point to a rabbit and you have pointed to a stage of a rabbit, to an integral part of a rabbit, to the rabbit fusion. . . . Point to an integral part of a rabbit and you have pointed again to the remaining [three] sorts of things; and so on around. Nothing not distinguished in stimulus meaning itself is to be distinguished by pointing, unless the pointing is accompanied by questions of identity and diversity; "Is this the same gavagai as that?" "Do we have here one gavagai or two?" (p. 53).

We take exception to Quine's basic argument. He argues that only by supplementing the pointing with questions about identity and diversity can we hope to interpret "gavagai," to decide what object(s) it really refers to. Perhaps he is correct. The other alternative, however, is that he has made the test conditions on which stimulus meaning depends more constrained, or weaker, than need be. It is possible that we can arrange test conditions as nonverbal as those of stimulus meaning but with far more diagnostic power, perhaps even as much power as Quine's questions about identity. To some degree this has already been done by psychologists interested in object constancy; in attempting to decide whether the human infant perceives "enduring objects" or "temporal segments" of objects, they are already sparring with two of Quine's alternatives, and with some success (see Bower 1974). Needless to say, the infants are not asked questions about identity and diversity, but are tested by methods every bit as nonverbal as those of stimulus meaning.

Consider two of Quine's alternatives: "*All* and *sundry* undetached parts of rabbits" and Goodman's *fusion* of all rabbits, "that single though discontinuous portion of the spatiotemporal world that consists of rabbits" (Goodman 1951). Are nonverbal tests truly unable to decide between these alternatives and rabbit as an enduring object?

Consider first "all and sundry undetached parts of rabbits." The difference here is between an object that never comes apart (unless acted upon by an external force) and one that freely separates into parts. In the latter case, the gavagai we saw is composed of parts that came together only a moment before being observed; it will fly apart again, and the next rabbit we behold may consist of the old head, a new torso, the old tail ("old" in the sense that only last week the head and tail had appeared together). That is, rabbit parts come "into and out of union" in the one case but remain fixed in the other case—that of the enduring object. Actually, this topic is the source of one of my favorite images, described below.

Picture two springboards or trampolines set across from each other. A figure mounts one of them, bounces a few times, and then launches himself toward the opposite board, crossing over by way of a simple flip, a swan dive, or something more elaborate. This procession of mounting, bouncing, and landing continues for a time, each new figure making the crossing without incident, until one of them comes apart in midflight. But he remains apart or disassembled for only a moment. As swiftly as the parts separate, they reunite, as though they had come apart only to demonstrate their cleverness, their knowledge of where each goes. Indeed, the parts complete their separation and reunion while in midair; the figure lands—perfectly reassembled.

The interest of this spectacle could be increased, no doubt, by varying the pieces into which the figure divides, but my own imagery is conservative. I stick closely to canonical pieces—heads, legs, arms, torsos, and the like—increasing interest by doubling the *number* of figures that jump and cross at the same time. Picture now, a pair of individuals—a man and a woman, a woman and a skeleton, a skeleton and a horse—each of them mounting one of the two opposing boards, each acknowledging the other with a slight smile or nod. The figures launch themselves at the same time, often using the same form of transit. Picture, if you will, two paunchy, middle-aged figures in simultaneous low-flying swan dives, passing one another in midair as they land on boards still trembling from the departure of the other figure. They too, as you would suppose, sometimes come apart in midflight, but reassemble before landing. Of course, the cases of greatest interest are those in which "pieces" from the two figures become scrambled in midair so that what lands on the opposite board is neither, say, man nor cow but "some" of each.

I have played this game in my head on a number of occasions, trying different combinations of items, not only of people and animals but also of vegetables, houses, and cars. The spectacle in my head is so amusing, such a delight, that I'm confident a videotape or motion-picture rendition would be widely enjoyed, producing smiles and even laughter in adults—perhaps a bit of fear in children. Which is my point. This videotape would have no effect on creatures whose conception of gavagai is of "all and sundry undetached parts of rabbits." It delights humans precisely because that is *not* our conception.

Lurking behind the multiplicity of interpretations that can be defended for *any* item to which the native might point or assent is, of course, the much deeper problem of induction or nondemonstrative inference, a problem to which Quine has contributed other keen examples. Perhaps most relevant for the psychologist is the mystery of how the child learns the meaning of any word. A mother points to a dog while saying "dog." How does the child learn that the intended referent is the animal rather than, say, its eye (to which the mother's finger points), the color, the movement of the eye (which blinks as the mother points), or even the number "one," of which the dog is a perfect exemplar?

The moment that Quine, Goodman (1965), Hempel (1965), and others spelled out this problem, psychologists were in their debt. For how often does one field hand another field a problem with so clear a set of guidelines for solution? Instructed by these guidelines, psychologists knew how to spend their time constructively, knew, for example, not to waste it by trying to build a learning device that would enable the child to sort through all logically possible alternatives before finally settling on the correct one. Instead, psychologists have delimited the set, have shown how it can be narrowed by constraints that are essentially genetic. The psychologists' constructive task was to discover the *nature* of the constraints.

Elizabeth Spelke (1984) shows uncommon common sense in suggesting that the human infant is constrained to perceive *objects* and in then attempting to determine experimentally what it is that infants perceive as objects. If perceiving objects is the proper constraint, how children associate "dog" *not* with the color, movement, eye, etc. of the dog but with the dog itself is no longer a mystery. Indeed, the mystery shifts: what additional constraints and systems enable the child (initially constrained to see objects) to learn names for *nonobjects*—colors, shapes, movements, numbers, and all the rest? (See Ellen Markman 1983 for interesting data and a different slant on this problem.)

Quine's "native" is, I assume, no different from the child in this respect; he too is constrained to perceive only some of the logically possible alternatives. As a result, our problem reduces to one of devising nonverbal tests that will uncover the native's constraints. Consider, as a last example, Nelson Goodman's rabbit fusion. Now there is, of course, such an "object" as the fusion of all rabbits, and when you point to an individual rabbit, you necessarily point to the fusion. But because the fusion is a real object, it hardly follows that the native, when pointing to the rabbit, recognizes that he is pointing to the fusion (or has the fusion in mind as his referent). Actually, I have difficulty picturing species that are constrained to perceive fusions, although I can think of two preoccupations that might incline a species to entertain this interpretation. One has to do with morality, the other with physics—with gravitational attraction. I will take up the former, describing how to determine whether or not a species holds the *moral* view and thus, when pointing to a rabbit, is likely to have the "fusion" in mind.

Goodman's fusion, "that single though discontinuous portion of the spatiotemporal world that consists of rabbits," is a conception that I did not recognize immediately. I knew I had "seen" it before, but it was a while before I could remember where. Then it became clear: Goodman's fusion is a physical model for a *moral* state or condition. The moral state is the one of which John Donne speaks in his famous *Meditation XVII*: "No man is an *Iland*, intire of it selfe; every man is a peece of the *Continent*, a part of the *maine* . . . any man's *death* diminishes *me*, because I am involved in *Mankinde*." It is a condition in which there is a connectedness (between all members of a category) that could express itself in a number of forms. For example, let us first establish, from an appropriate aerial view, the space-time distribution of all rabbits. We then kill one of the rabbits and directly test a selected sample of the remaining members of the category for grief—"grief" being defined as a specific kind of deflection from base condition. Suppose we find that grief increases in inverse proportion to the distance between the victim and the remaining members of the category. We need not demonstrate anything more. That is, it is not required, in order to judge the appropriateness of Goodman's "fusion" as a model for moral connectedness, that we specify the mechanism by which grief is propagated. Nevertheless, it is clear even from the first round of data that standard sensation and perception could not possibly be the mechanism of propagation. Increased grief is noted in rabbits too distant to have observed either the killing of the victim or the disturbance produced in other rabbits that were close enough to have observed the killing. The perturbation comes simply from connectedness, from membership in the same category. That is to say, natural categories are not the artifacts—the classification devices—that some have supposed. They are natural parts of the world, and as natural parts, they have a *moral* force (quite as natural parts have a *gravitational* force).

Goodman's fusion is an apt physical model for Donne's connectedness; people who do and do not believe in this moral view will respond differently to appropriate visual events. Suppose we prepare the following videotapes: a spatial-temporal distribution of cups viewed from an aerial perspective, a similar view of pumpkins, of zebras. We break one of the cups (crush one of the pumpkins, shoot one of the zebras) and observe perturbation ripple through each category. Cups tremble and show stress lines, pumpkins fracture, zebras stumble in inverse proportion to the distance between the class member and the member victimized. Believers (in the moral view) and non-believers alike will react differently to these videotapes, so we may infer their interpretation of "gavagai" from these differences.

To translate a word, and thus escape the indeterminacy of translation that Quine alleges to exist, we have only to combine the information provided by these tests with that provided by the stimulus meaning of a word used as an occasion sentence. These two pieces of information will enable us to specify both the conditions that occasion a word and the interpretation the native puts on the conditions. This, in turn, will enable us to specify the items to which a word refers and thus to state the extension of the word (not only its stimulus meaning).

Consider another type of procedure, no less behavioral than the first, that could also be used to establish conceptual scheme. Though less direct, I discuss it because there is a considerable advantage in having two procedures. If the two procedures are genuinely different operations and give the same answer, we can put more stock in their convergence than in an answer given by either one alone.

In this second procedure, we delay attempting to translate the native's words, and try instead to *teach* him some words (bringing the native closer to the chimpanzee and the linguist's task closer to our own). We concentrate on that small set of words Quine has identified as being indispensable in attempting to diagnose the native's conceptual scheme. The set includes such distinctions as this/that, singular/plural, identity/non-identity, not the English words, of course, but the native's equivalent (which, as Quine notes, may or may not be in one-to-one correspondence with English). Just these distinctions are needed to formulate questions that Quine proposes the linguist ask of the native in order to "get at his conceptual scheme": "Is this the same gavagai as that?" or "Do we have here one gavagai or two?"

We were able to teach the chimpanzee many of the distinctions, all those that we tried in fact, including this/that (Premack 1976, p. 281), singular/plural (p. 225), and the quantifiers "all, none, one, several" (p. 268). We did not use the words to formulate those questions about identity and diversity that Quine says will help decipher the native's conceptual structure (of course, we cannot be confident that an ape could be asked such questions); but such a course may not be necessary. An individual's conceptual scheme may be revealed simply in his ability, or inability, to acquire labels for the distinctions in question.

Consider the demonstrative adjectives "this" and "that." Like the pronouns "you" and "me," they involve a distinction that is defined relative to the speaker: "this" refers to items proximal to the speaker, "that" to items distal to the speaker. Because of this complexity it was of interest to determine whether or not apes could learn such words (the successful acquisition of "you/me" in sign does not answer the question, the distinction being based on iconic gestures—the speaker simply points either to himself or to his listener). Sarah acquired the basic distinction (Premack 1976, p. 281), but there are further subtleties in the human distinction that we did not examine. We are concerned here, however, not with the complexities of words defined relative to the speaker, but with what the distinction may presuppose about the perceived character of the objects modified by the distinction.

Picture our "native" receiving the same language lessons as the chimpanzees. The trainer arranges two rabbits, one closer to the native than the other, so that their location qualifies them as objects to be modified by "this/that." We require of the native, as we did of the chimpanzee, that in requesting *rabbits* he refer to them as "this" or "that," in keeping with the definition of the terms; whereas in responding to requests made of him to "take this rabbit" or "take that rabbit," he must observe whatever changes in rabbit that a change in speaker entails.

The native differs from the chimpanzee, let us suppose, in that he does not regard rabbits as enduring objects. They are, for him, in continual flux—parts of the proximal one being exchanged with parts of the distal, not to mention a lesser exchange between more remote rabbits and those at hand. Can he acquire "this/that" nonetheless, later using these words as we do? Or will his conceptual scheme interfere with this acquisition?

He should be able to acquire some version of "this/that," it would seem, but a version different from ours. Where we use "this/that" to modify objects, he would use these words to modify locations, for it is the locations and not the objects that "endure" in his conceptual scheme. His difficulty in learning to distinguish "this rabbit" and "that rabbit" should contrast with his ease in learning to distinguish "this place" and "that place," and this peculiar and unexpected contrast may alert us to the peculiarity in his conceptual scheme.

Notice that a native, slow to acquire "this/that" as a modifier of certain objects, may nevertheless readily acquire these labels as modifiers of *other* objects. Suppose that rabbits, for the "native" in question, are not infinitely divisible, but have atomic constituents. In fact, for this native, who is only a step removed from us, atomic rabbit parts are head, body, legs, and the like. In teaching the native "this/that," we need only to substitute these *stable* atoms for the *unstable* molecular wholes in order to bring about normal learning. If, on the other hand, the native were more than a step removed from us and had no atomic constituents in his conceptual scheme, had only the ability to divide every part into still further parts, we should then find no differences in rate of learning. He should be as obtuse in learning to apply "this/that" to any part we might use as in learning to apply the distinction to that larger object from which the parts were taken. This difference itself could serve to distinguish between atomists and nonatomists, the Heraclitean and non-Heraclitean native, and tell us something about conceptual scheme as well. Admittedly, the degrees of freedom here seem large, so that the chance of using these differences to decipher conceptual scheme may appear remote. I daresay that once some research has been done, the degrees of freedom will appear more normal. In the meantime, I do not propose the use of this approach by itself to diagnose conceptual scheme but suggest it as a supplement to other procedures. What would count is a convergence in the several approaches.

Quine actually makes things too easy for the linguist by arranging for a "native" whose dispositions are entirely familiar and who, it would appear, names everything we name. What if, although naming what we name, the native assigns different interpretations to that which he names? We could not diagnose these possible differences if we confined ourselves to the weak test conditions that are entailed by "stimulus meaning." We can, as Quine arranges it, decipher these possible differences in interpretation only by using appropriate words. The words are not available to us, however, for they are of a kind that cannot be established on the basis of "stimulus meaning"; hence, Quine's thesis for the indeterminacy of translation.

If we strengthen the behavioral tests, we can, as already argued, get rid of interpretive ambiguity; for example, nonverbal tests can tell us whether "gavagai" and "rabbit" are coextensive. But truly alien species would name items different from those we name, and the differences could be of such a nature as to prevent the linguist from getting off the ground. As one example, consider the native who (like Quine's) says, "gavagai" whenever a rabbit appears. It looks as though "gavagai" equals "rabbit" again. Not until there is an accidental change in the observers, however, does the linguist discover "gavagai" could not possibly mean rabbit. On this occasion, both linguist and native happen to be standing in the brush (concealed from the rabbit's view) when a child *and* a rabbit appear. The native now says "plengi."

What happened to "gavagai"? "Gavagai" departed with the departure of the two adults (the native and the linguist) from the rabbit's field of vision. We erroneously construed "gavagai" and other occasion sentences to be the "names of things." These natives do not "name things" (under any definition of "things"). What they name instead are inferences: what they *believe* to be the interpretation that an "object" (we thought was a "name") would make of what it observes. For instance, "gavagai" does not mean "rabbit" but something like "hated hunter" or "oppressor"—the description that the native believes the rabbit would assign to adults (himself and the linguist)—while "plengi" means "fellow sufferer" or "small victim"—the description the native believes that the rabbit reserves for the young child. Here, then, is a species for which stimulus meaning is not to be discovered principally by changing the canonically construed stimulating condition, but by changing the observer.

Rather than multiply possibilities, turn to a case closer to home—Quine's interpretation of truth functions and how they are likely to apply to the chimpanzee. Quine treats truth functions as a logician naturally would, as devices for connecting sentences. Thus the semantic criterion for conjunction is that it produce compounds to which "one is prepared to assent always and only when one is prepared to assent to each component," where the components are occasion sentences (1960, p. 58). This treatment is inadequate for our purposes, however, since it assumes what we cannot assume, that the use and comprehension of logical connectives deals exclusively with sentences (rather than with something more fundamental). We need to raise a different question: What are the stimulations (in Quine's idiom) that the individual would interpret as instances of conjunction, disjunction, etc.? To find out, we offer our subject not sentences but scenes from the world and ask which of them he would represent separately and which in a unified way.

For example, we show the ape two containers in a field, about six meters apart and allow him to observe that the first contains apples, the other bananas. Later, testing reveals that he not only remembers the content of both containers, but also remembers them in a connected fashion (one that might be formulated as: "A contains apple and B contains banana"). That A and B are linked is demonstrated when the ape matches A and B, even when equivalent alternatives are present; that is, by satiating him on apples (but not bananas), he goes to B rather than C (which also contains bananas); and by satiating him on bananas (but not apples), he goes to A but not D (which also contains apples).

We find, however, that if we show him the two containers at different times, say, A in the morning and B in the evening, the two are not represented in his memory in a connected manner. Although he remembers both A and B, just as well as he remembers them when they were shown to him in the same or adjacent intervals of time, they are not represented as a unit. For example, given satiation tests, he performs in a quite different way: satiated on apples, he is no more likely to seek bananas in B than in C; satiated on bananas, no more likely to seek apples in A than in D.

Tests of this kind, dealing *not* with sentences but with conditions in the world, ask whether potentially distinct pieces of information are likely to be represented in a joint fashion or not. "Joint" is not, of course, equivalent to conjunction (though it would be a great surprise if the two were unrelated). To determine what the relation between them may be, we arrange tests of the sort Quine proposes, first establishing the animal's agreement to each of several components and then presenting them together for the animal's assent or dissent.

Suppose we find that the animal will not assent to many of the combined occasion sentences, even though it assents to them individually. For example, when we try "gavagai" and "natilu," the animal dissents, even though assenting to each individually. The stimulus meanings of "gavagai" and "natilu" are, as it turns out, "rabbit" and "umbrella," respectively. The animal will not, perhaps cannot, in any case does not assent to "Lo, a rabbit and an umbrella." Neither, let us suppose, will the ape assent to "apple in A and banana in B" when the two pieces of information were made known to him at widely separate times of day.

In applying to other species tests that Quine recommends we may be shown how immensely peculiar humans are. We may be the only species either willing or able to conjunct any multiple of sentences to which we assent individually. All other species may treat conjunction more restrictively. For them, assent to individual sentences may be a necessary but not sufficient condition for assent to their conjunction. This would not mean (and Quine would be among the first to point it out) that the logic of these species differs at all from human logic. It would mean only that the occasions on which they use their logic may be far more restricted than those of humans.

Interrogation: Linguistic and Nonlinguistic

Commenting thirteen years after *Word and Object*, Quine regretted that "gavagai" had figured so centrally in the discussion of the indeterminacy of translation (1973). The deep basis of the doctrine was not the "inscrutability of terms," the "gavagai" example, but nothing less than the fact that theories are underdetermined by evidence, physical theory no less than linguistic. Assent to the indeterminacy of science appears to be virtually universal (thanks in no small part to Quine); and I have no need to disturb the universality, for my concern here is not with that issue but a different one. I am concerned with the implications of Quine's position for the study of comparative intelligence, for what we can establish about the mind of the "other one." The tables are now turned, the inscrutability of terms counting for more than the indeterminacy of science.

Quine's position is important for the study of comparative intelligence because it makes language, the capacity for interrogation, the essential condition for the nontrivial understanding of the other one. He not only limits what can be established between two individuals who share a language, but also sets additional (and severe) limits on what can be established when individuals do not share a language. The limits concern the denotation of terms and the claim that these can be established only through interrogation.

Since we shall never be able to interrogate most of the species of this world, if Quine's position were correct, there would be painfully little we could know about the minds of most of the inhabitants of this world. Guided by the gavagai example, we could catalogue the responses of different species, identifying the stimulus conditions in each case. In addition, we could refine our physical analysis of these conditions. Does the native, when offered a rabbit which is blue, five-legged, the size of an ant— which slinks rather than jumps, continue to utter "gavagai"? Moreover, in carrying out our physical analyses we need not be restricted to the macro-level. Proceeding from macro to micro, we could establish, in addition, the chemical formula of the stimulus condition for the copulatory response in an ant. What we could not do, however, is move in the opposite direction: refine our conceptual analysis of the stimulus condition.

As long as the individual was noninterrogable, we could not determine how it interpreted its stimulus conditions—more important, whether it interpreted them at all. Do species differ in the degree to which they interpret stimulus conditions, with some lacking the capacity altogether, others having the capacity and making interpretations, still others not only making interpretations but also being conscious of them, as appears to be the case with our species? Quine's position would make this question unanswerable. Admittedly, his position does not err, as others seem to do (see Schwartz 1978) by making the very act of interpretation depend on language. Yet his position would lock us into a permanent agnosticism with respect to this and related questions.

Is interrogation our only means of interpreting the stimulus conditions of others? I have already suggested otherwise, sketching nonlinguistic procedures that can be substituted when interrogation is not a possibility. I will now enlarge upon the sketch, giving a fuller account of the nonlinguistic alternatives. In order to do so I take a major human interpretation, causality, and ask whether it could be detected in languageless or noninterrogable species. Our first inclination with cases of this kind is to ask the evolutionary question: Did the interpretation arise de novo with our species or are its roots to be found elsewhere? Our concern here is not with that question, however, but with a comparison between interrogation and what I shall propose as its nonlinguistic surrogate. I want to establish why the non-linguistic alternative works at all, why it has some resolving power, though less than that of language. Interrogation *is* our most effective way of interpreting the stimulus conditions of others. Why, exactly?

Causality has several aspects. Let us start with the transformation that is the main expression or manifestation of causal action in the physical domain. An individual makes a change in either the state and/or location of an object, generally with the use of an instrument. For instance, he moves a chair or paints a wall. To determine whether a child understands this transformation, we might place a whole apple to one side, halves of an apple to the other, and ask "what caused this change?" If the child pointed to the knife (rather than to the pencil or container of water), we would be encouraged; we would be even more so if, when we replaced the apples with a dry sponge and a wet one, the child replaced the knife with the container of water and continued with appropriate replacements for all the changes we made.

As it turns out, we need not have asked the child *anything*. The same evidence can be obtained by pretending that the child is speechless or noninterrogable. Present the same sequences as before, for example, apple-blank-cut apples, along with the same alternatives (knife, pencil, container of water), and say nothing. The child will make the same choices. More important for our purpose, so will the chimpanzee; that is, if we test the ape in the same way as the "noninterrogable" child, we obtain the same results (Premack 1976).

Apple-blank-cut apples, sponge-blank-wet sponge, paper-blank-marked paper—these and all other cases we can give the ape or child patently differ from the linguistic sequence "what caused this change?" Yet in the child both sequences evoke the same response, and the ape responds to the *nonlinguistic* sequences in the same way as the child. What do the two kinds of sequences have in common so that they elicit the same responses?

The nonlinguistic sentence is, I suggest, an implicit question for the same reason that, say, "blank is Popeye's favorite food" or "Washington was the blank president of the United States" is an explicit question. Both kinds of sequences can be seen as incomplete versions of something that can be made complete. I do not, of course, claim that all questions are incomplete sequences; I claim the opposite. When an individual can foresee or imagine a complete sequence within the incomplete one he is given, the sequence—whether composed of words or of objects—has the force of a question, and a response to it can be treated as an answer.

This same argument permits us to see why actual interrogation has the resolving power lacking in the nonlinguistic counterpart. Although it is our intention when presenting the ape or child with, say, apple-blank-cut apples, to ask "what caused this change?", the individual may not interpret the nonlinguistic structure as dealing specifically with *cause*. He may see the sequence as asking merely what is associated with apples? what is as "cuttable" as apples? as round? as red? and so forth. The word "cause" in the explicit question immediately eliminates all these unintended alternatives.

The nonlinguistic case is by no means hopeless, however. The results often resolve much of the ambiguity. For instance, an individual who consistently chooses the correct instrument for each transformation shown would eliminate most of the competing options. An alternative that would remain, however, is that the individual, though choosing correctly, does not regard the instruments as causes but as mere associates of the transformations. Not even that alternative is impregnable. Suppose the individual has never written on apples, cut sponges, or wet paper. Nonetheless, he chooses instruments that are appropriate to these anomalous transformations rather than others that have long been associated with the objects in question. These are, in fact, the results we obtained with the apes (Premack 1976), permitting us to reject the associative hypothesis. Does that settle the matter, then, and finally clear the field of all contenders, leaving the causality hypothesis the only survivor? Hardly. We are permanently consigned to picturing alternatives and running controls to eliminate them (while at the same time welcoming graciously from critics those we have overlooked). Is *this* a novel predicament?

The nonlinguistic approach to the interpretation of stimulus conditions simply faces the usual problems of science: we strengthen one hypothesis while weakening others (or reading Popper (1972) strictly, do nothing but weaken alternatives). Although Quine regards the indeterminacy of translation to hold over and above normal scientific indeterminacy, I have difficulty with his argument. The indeterminacy of psychology, as illustrated by our present example, would seem to be the indeterminacy of normal science.

The nonlinguistic approach is not restricted to the causality interpretation; we could take the same approach to intention and belief, that is, to the possibility that we are not the only species attributing states of mind to others (Premack and Woodruff 1978). There, too, we present the individual with incomplete nonlinguistic sequences or sequences that can be seen in this light by the mind endowed with appropriate interpretive capacity. The sequences differ from those used in the causality tests only in that they are dynamic rather than static, videotapes rather than simple displays of objects.

Specifically, we show apes and young children videotapes in which an individual (an actor) appears to be struggling to obtain food that is inaccessible. The videotapes are accompanied by photographic alternatives depicting different modes of solving the problem, for example, by stepping up onto a chair (when food is out of reach on the vertical) or reaching out with a stick (when it is out of reach on the horizontal) and so forth.

Individuals who consistently choose solutions would appear to have perceived problems, that is, to have interpreted the videotapes as showing an individual who *wants* certain outcomes and *believes* that by acting in certain ways he could achieve them. Sarah, our most talented ape, and children older than about three and a half consistently choose solutions (Premack and Woodruff 1978). Younger children and apes younger than Sarah do not. Rather than solutions, they tend to choose photographs resembling some salient item in the videotape, for example, a yellow bird because it is yellow like the bananas in the videotape. When an individual chooses in this manner, on the basis of physical resemblance, we have no grounds for claiming that he perceives a problem or, indeed, makes any interpretation at all. On the contrary, for such an individual the videotape would appear to consist of a sequence of uninterpreted events. Needless to say, the defense of this attributional interpretation demands a set of controls—even greater than the one demanded for the defense of the causality interpretation, but not different in principle from those demanded for the defense of any scientific hypothesis.

In the causality example we celebrated the advantages of true interrogation. The word "cause" in the question "what caused this change?" directed the listener to one interpretation, as opposed to the many that seem possible with nonlinguistic "questions." How impressively the linguistic question parries the ambiguity that engulfs its nonlinguistic counterpart. We must now, however, ask how the child acquired the word "cause" and other words like it. How did the child manage to associate with "cause" exactly the intended interpretation and not the many others that seem possible (some of which only recently figured in our discussion of the nonlinguistic approach to causal interpretation)? Were controls of any sort run by the child's caretakers to cope with the child's possible misconstruals? We need not claim, of course, that the specific corrections a parent may make of a child's misconstruals will be equivalent to the controls that must be included in the scientific test. There are several reasons why the two would be expected to differ. Yet, when language is first acquired, if controls of sorts are needed to assure univocal interpretation, how radical is the difference between linguistic and nonlinguistic interrogation? Timing would seem to be the main difference. We have a choice: either to run the controls *early* during language acquisition or *later*, at the time of the scientific test.

Noninterrogable Cases

For species that cannot be reached by interrogation, linguistic or otherwise, we can substitute habituation, using it to identify not only stimulus conditions but also, within limits, their interpretations.

For instance, we can test the causality case in this fashion, taking advantage of the work of Albert Michotte (1963), the Belgian psychologist who devoted years to establishing the determinants of causal interpretation in the human adult. Subtleties aside, Michotte showed that the determinants are basically no more than spatial and temporal contiguity. For example, when the human observes one ball strike another, provided there is spatial and temporal contiguity between the collision and the subsequent movement of the second ball, the human regards the first ball as causing the movement of the second. Interestingly, if temporal and spatial contiguity are violated, then despite repeated "collisions" between the two balls, all of them resulting in the movement of the second one, the human observer does not perceive causality. Indeed, he denies that the relation between the two balls is causal. Hume's supposition that human belief in causality results from the repeated association between two events is already questioned by this finding and could be questioned further by duplicating the outcome with infants (who lack adult experience with repeated associations of any kind). The implications of Michotte's findings are these: human belief in causality does not arise from repeated experience, but simply from perceiving a visual configuration of a special kind. We have only to see this configuration *once* to experience the sensation of causality. Conversely, if the configuration is not present, despite the association of two events, you will not experience the sensation of causality.

Are languageless creatures—infants, apes, rats, pigeons, etc.—responsive to the stimulus conditions of causality? Relying on Michotte's findings, we show the individual, repeatedly, an example of a causal relation—a configuration the human adult would describe in causal terms—until he habituates or loses interest in looking at the example. Then we attempt to restore his interest using two kinds of cases: one that is an example of a causal relation, and one that is not (both of which differ equally in their physical composition from the first example). Suppose that the former produces very little release from habituation, whereas the latter restores the original looking times. In other words, suppose there is perfect accord between those cases human observers describe in causal terms and those that do not restore the looking times of our languageless observers; likewise, suppose perfect accord between those cases that human observers do not describe in causal terms and those that do restore the looking times of our observers. Would we not then credit the languageless creatures with being responsive to the stimulus conditions of causality?

These results would leave us basically unfulfilled, however. Our real interest is not in the stimulus condition but rather in the interpretation. And the habituation test would not tell us, for instance, whether in responding to the Michottean configuration, the rat makes the inductive leap—assumes that outcomes observed to occur once will recur whenever the original conditions are reinstated. We can take further steps: present the rat with conditions that violate the Michottean configuration—for example, perfect "collisions" that do not result in movement of the impacted body. The rat, let us suppose, appears discomfitted or startled or has a protracted looking time. But does this prove that rats make mental as well as physical leaps? Any perfect "collision" that failed to yield a normal outcome should produce discomfiture. Proof of the inductive leap may require further evidence: the rat must show greater discomfiture with failed "collisions" that had already succeeded once.

It seems almost certain that we share stimulus classes with many species; consider, for example, those we appear to share with the pigeon, viz. people, tree, water, and the like (Herrnstein, Loveland, and Cable 1976). Unfortunately, we do not yet know how deep the sharing may go. Since not even partial physical analyses have been carried out for either pigeon or human, we cannot say whether the ingredients of these classes, or the formula according to which they are combined, are the same for the two species (though see Cerella 1982 for instructive attempts at physical analysis). Indeed, we do not know what relation the bird may see between representation and reality. If shown pictures of Jane "feeding" and Jack "beating" pigeons, would the bird, upon encountering the actual persons, immediately seek Jane and/or shun Jack? Nor can we say what interpretations, if any, the bird makes of its stimulus classes. Does it anticipate certain properties when it perceives people, a different set of properties when it perceives water, and still others when it perceives trees—properties that in all cases go beyond those that can be perceived in the stimulus conditions? A positive answer would make the bird an interpretative species; an unreservedly negative one would deny knowledge or interpretation to the pigeon, making of it mainly a perceptual species.

Chimpanzees show recognition of superordinate classes, discriminating animal from nonanimal and fruit from nonfruit (Premack 1976, p. 220; Wheeler and Premack, unpublished data), but here too, we have neither physical nor conceptual analysis of the classes. When the ape places a horse with a dog (rather than an apple) and an apple with a banana (rather than a dog), does it know, or rather is it capable of learning, that members of one category begin as flowers and members of the other develop within the body of another animal? Perhaps we can find out by presenting the ape with scenes that do and do not conflict with human interpretations; for example, apples growing on a tree in one case and on an animal's body in another. Or we might determine which sequence would be more likely to startle the ape: one in which a neonatal ape turned into a juvenile that became an adult ape, or one in which a nest turned into a tulip that became a dog. Perhaps even if apes do not attain human levels of interpretation, their expectations may be guided by certain principles, for example, by a principle of "homogeneous transformation": a small ape that turns into a larger one may be more acceptable than an apple that turns into an ape, and the principle may even be directional, "small" turning into "large" more acceptably than "large" into "small."

Children, when very young, may not be startled by apples that grow from the body of a horse or trees on which small horses are seen to be growing like apples. But to find such scenes incongruous, they have only to acquire appropriate knowledge—we know that they can acquire it. We do not know whether the chimpanzee can. Perhaps the animal cannot make interpretations that depend on historical process such as the growth of plants or the development of animals. They may be restricted to interpretation based on the anticipation of sensory qualities. From the exterior of a fruit, for example, the ape may foresee the interior—pulp, juiciness, seeds, sweetness, but not the history—the seed that grew into a tree that developed a bloom that became an orange and so forth. If there are limits on the knowledge that nonhuman species can acquire, we cannot yet state these limits with any precision, or relate them to possible mechanisms of the mind.

Class Inclusion and Functional Analysis

Simply because it can match one animal with another or one fruit with another we cannot conclude that the ape understands class inclusion (and has information organized in its mind in a hierarchical manner). The heart of class inclusion is the asymmetrical, transitive relation that holds between superordinate and subordinate classes. For example, all horses are animals (as all oranges are fruit), but the reverse is not true; not all animals are horses (nor are all fruit oranges). Does the ape grasp this essential asymmetry? Only if it does so can it be said to understand class inclusion.

Perhaps we could settle the matter by interrogating the animal, asking it, for example, "? all oranges fruit" (are all oranges fruit?) and "? all fruit oranges," since the animal can acquire all the words on which these questions depend. For instance, the animal can be taught the quantifiers, correctly "describing" sets consisting of four items as, for example, "one cracker square" (one of four crackers is square), "all cracker square," "some cracker square" (more than one but less than all crackers are square), and "none cracker square" (Premack 1976, p. 268). In addition, the ape can be taught names of classes—"fruit," "candy"—not to mention names of class members (Premack 1976, p. 228). Unfortunately, however, answering questions about class inclusion (or any other topic) requires more than understanding the individual words comprising the questions.

If the animal cannot answer the questions, shall we conclude that it does not understand class inclusion? Or can we take refuge in the possibility that the question was not well framed? If we put the question in a simpler way, will the ape be able to answer it? We cannot cling to this alternative, however, for I can find no way to simplify the question; further, I can find no nonlinguistic procedure to substitute for the question.

It is not possible, as far as I can see, to construct nonlinguistic examples of the asymmetrical relation between superordinate and subordinate classes. The most that can be demonstrated nonlinguistically is that the animal can sort objects at increasingly abstract levels, for example, place apples with apples, fruit with fruit, even food or edibles with food. But does the animal grasp that while food encompasses fruit, fruit does not encompass food? Unfortunately, the grasp of class inclusion is no more demonstrated by higher-level than by lower-level sorting.

Fortunately, other aspects of knowledge, no less deep than that of class inclusion, can be represented on a nonlinguistic basis. Consider, for example, functional analysis. A certain aspect of behavior is caused by or is a function of an external condition and varies in magnitude with the variation in magnitude of the condition. Take the simple case of a dog burying a bone. The duration of that act will vary with several conditions, principally with the vigor of the dog, hardness of the soil, size of the bone, and the like. Does the dog know that? Can it use knowledge in its problem solving?

The dog, we may assume, has buried many bones, always doing a good job. The hole it digs suits the dimensions of the bone: the dog does not try to force large bones into little holes or wastefully construct large holes for little bones. The dog also covers the hole properly, not with a fixed number of strokes but with the right amount of soil. All this affirms that the dog is a relatively plastic species (not a reflex-dominated one), capable of making nice adjustments to a changing world. But it would not answer the question of whether the dog has made a functional analysis of bone burial. Does the dog know, as someone who has made a functional analysis would, that if vigor and soil are held constant, bone size then becomes the main determinant of how long it takes to bury a bone? Fortunately, we can find out with the use of nonlinguistic tests—"fortunately," since it is unlikely that we shall ever be able to talk to dogs.

We make an observer of a hungry dog by restraining it, while at the same time allowing it to watch two other dogs burying bones. The observer can see everything except the bones themselves. For example, it can see that the two dogs (of about equal size) dig at about the same rate (in fact, they dig in unison) and that the soil they throw back is the same; yet it takes one dog twice as long to finish as the other. When the two dogs finish and depart, we release the hungry observer. Where does it go? Suppose it goes unhesitatingly to the location where one of the dogs labored much longer than the other. And it does this not only in the one case but in all cases, despite variation in dogs, time, places, and the like. Such an outcome, however unlikely, would suggest that the dog has made a functional analysis, and we would do well to arrange other tests that could support the conclusion more decisively.

4

The Dependence of Language on Nonlanguage Factors

In this section we look at two topics that are hardly more related than goats and Wall Street. Why then put temporal discrimination and emotion, our next two topics, in the same section? Because relative to language they do have one thing in common. Although neither is an intrinsic part of language, both are related to it—temporal discrimination as a component on which language may depend, emotion as a complex process whose relationship to language is still in part mysterious.

Temporal Order

Recipes for human language are somewhat like those for dinosaur stew—long, heterogeneous, and necessarily a bit vague. For example, "a predisposition to communicate, an ability to mimic sound, the intelligence to learn and to label and relate classes of objects and events, and a sensitivity to differences in the sequences of signs," if we take our recipe from George Miller (1983, p. 31), a slightly different set of ingredients if we borrow from other experts (e.g., Hockett 1960). In addition, most experts view the combination, and not the individual ingredients themselves, as the mark of uniqueness in the human species—"an enormously improbable evolutionary accident," in Miller's words. A prominent example of a nonexclusive ingredient on the phonological level is an inner ear structure enabling the categorical discrimination of sounds, a structure demonstrated not only in humans but also in the chinchilla (Kuhl and Miller 1975) and rhesus monkey (Waters and Wilson 1976).

How, in fact, does the ape stand with respect to the recipe for human language? Suppose we found the ape to lack many of the ingredients in the recipe? The absence of language in the ape would then comply with a view assigning language to a certain level of intelligence, a level corresponding more or less to the number of items on the list. On the other hand, if the ape were to possess every competence on the list, and still not have language, we would require a substantially different point of view.

In this section we turn to one ingredient, Miller's "sensitivity to differences in the sequences of signs." The discrimination of order, especially temporal order, has long been viewed as a human specialization, so much so that some writers (e.g., Hebb and Thompson 1968) have denied language to nonhumans specifically on the grounds of incompetence in temporal order.

From the ape's success in discriminating between strings of words differing only in order, for example, "red on green," versus "green on red" (Premack 1976, p. 107), we already know that it can discriminate order. But that is spatial order: can the ape also discriminate temporal order? If so, how do the two compare? Further, if it can discriminate both temporal and spatial order, can it translate one into the other; that is, the order of time into the order of space, and vice versa? If so, at what cost? Finally, is the animal's ability to discriminate order confined to the sensory level or can it also discriminate order on the conceptual level? In answering this family of questions, we characterize the ape's general resources for analyzing order; we could then consider these resources to be available for combination with a linguistic factor, were such a factor ever to be added to the ape.

We tested Sarah not on sentences, meaningful combinations of words, but on sequences composed of nonsense elements

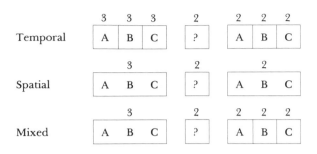

Figure 1

cut from colored paper. The elements were produced by factorially combining six shapes and four colors, making a total of twenty-four different elements. These elements were arranged in sequences of three and presented on the horizontal—first one sequence, then an interrogative particle, and then the second sequence. Of course, the two sequences in any pair always consisted of the same three elements and differed only in order (if they differed at all). The sequences were videotaped and presented to Sarah on a television monitor. Her task was to judge the sameness or difference of the order of the two sequences, using her plastic words "same" and "different."

To test her ability to discriminate temporal order, we presented the elements in each sequence and then removed them successively, as depicted in figure 1. All the elements appeared in the same location on the monitor. Each element in the first sequence appeared for three seconds and in the second sequence for two seconds. An interrogative particle was interposed between the two sequences and remained for two seconds. This mode of presentation affords no spatial information concerning order; order is strictly temporal. After the last element of the second sequence disappeared from the screen, the plastic words "same" and "different" were made available to Sarah, and she judged the two sequences by placing one of the words in a designated place.

In the spatial format, which is also depicted in figure 1, each sequence was presented simultaneously rather than successively.

The whole first sequence was shown for three seconds; it was replaced for two seconds by the interrogative particle; and this was replaced in turn (for two seconds) by the whole second sequence. Following the removal of the second sequence, the words "same" and "different" were again made available to Sarah, and she used them as she had in the previous case. The two kinds of trials (and yet a third kind, described below) were given in the same sessions, counterbalanced for order.

Sarah performed well above chance on both formats, 32 of 42 trials correct for the temporal case and 34 of 42 trials correct for the spatial case ($p < .001$ in both cases). Despite the differences in exposure duration and in duration of delay, differences that favored the temporal case in some respects and the spatial in others, she performed at approximately the same level in both cases, about 78 percent correct.

Given her success in judging both temporal and spatial order, it was of interest to determine whether she could translate the one kind of order into the other, and if she could, what the translation might cost her. To answer this question, we had only to present one of the two sequences in the temporal (or spatial) format and then present the other sequence in the alternate format. On half the trials the first sequence was temporal, the second spatial; on the other half this order was reversed, the two kinds of trials being counterbalanced over trials. In 84 trials of this kind, Sarah was correct 57 times ($p < .001$), with only a negligible difference between the time-space and space-time conditions. Thus, the ape can translate one kind of order into the other, though not entirely without cost. She was consistently about 10 percent less accurate on the mixed or translation cases than on the pure cases (Premack and Woodruff, in preparation).

The ape, therefore, can discriminate both temporal and spatial order and can translate one into the other with moderate cost. These results are compatible with the earlier language work showing that the ape can respond differentially to strings of words differing only in their order. The results are restricted, however, to order on the physical or sensory level; we should like to know whether the ape can also deal with order on a conceptual level. There are numerous ways to find out.

For example, we might construct sequences consisting of parts of fruit—seeds, stems, patches of colors, outlines of shape—given what we know to be the ape's mental representation of fruit. Suppose one sequence consisted of seed, color, wedge of fruit and another sequence of shape outline, stem, taste. The task is to decide whether the order of the two sequences is the same or different. The two sequences are obviously not physically alike, yet after a moment's thought we decide "same" because both sequences are cases of apple, banana, orange, respectively. Another sequence of essentially the same kind could consist not of fruit but of items of clothing, for example, glove, hat, shoes ? tie, coat, shirt. We rely now not on inalienable possession, the relation between a body and its parts, but on alienable possession, the relation between an individual and what he owns. Anyone familiar with the clothes and the individuals to whom they belong should recognize the sequence, physical differences aside, as a case of "same"; that is, as a case of Tom, Dick, Harry ? Tom, Dick, Harry.

The kind of conceptual sequences we gave Sarah were of still a different type. An example is LL GG XY ? AA BB CD, where the letters stand for common household items with which Sarah was highly familiar. The answer to this question is "same" since the sequence in both cases is *same, same, different*. A small rearrangement of the elements, for example, LL GG AA ? XY BB CD, produces the question for which the answer is "different" since now the sequence in one case is *same, same, same* while in the other it is *different, same, different*. Sarah passed tests of this kind at a respectable level of accuracy, 79 percent correct, though she did not do so immediately. It took considerable trial and error to find the limiting conditions under which she could pass tests of this kind. They were appreciably more restrictive than those for sensory or physical order and consisted of these conditions: spatial order, both sequences present at the same time (so that she was not required to remember either), and elements that were not videotapes but actual objects. It is possible, even likely, that with additional training she could be adapted to less restrictive conditions. But at least for these restricted conditions she was successful in judging conceptual order, 79 percent correct, a level comparable to her judgment for sensory order.

If we puzzle why the chimpanzee is not a missing linguistic link, not a species with an intermediate language, it cannot be because it lacks one of the competences needed in a combination of competences to yield language. Instead, despite a well-developed competence for order, the ape does not have language. The more abilities of this kind we can add to the list, the more can we defend the assertion that language is not simply a propitious assemblage of individual abilities but a competence in its own right. We have a long way to go, of course, before being able to defend such a claim. The present work gives some indication of what must be done in order to make such an argument appealing.

Emotion and Words

Our grasp of the connection between emotion and language in humans is gravely incomplete—in part because our understanding of human emotion is inadequate—but the profundity of the connection is beyond doubt. Indeed, the connection is so formidable that we are inclined to cloak its true magnitude in deceptive aphorisms. For instance, where is there greater trumpery than in "Sticks and stones may break my bones, but names will never hurt me"? For every ten people who lie in bed moaning from physical wounds, hundreds more quietly walk the streets, seething under the impact of a tongue lashing or some other form of verbally inflicted wound. The deep pain and no less exalted pleasure (consider the effect of "I love you" from the right mouth) that can be inflicted by human words and sentences attest to how profoundly human language and emotion are connected.

Does a similar connection hold between the words and emotions of the language-trained ape? Can words or sentences arouse in the ape, as they do so powerfully in humans, the emotions aroused by nonlinguistic means? At the risk of getting ahead of our story, I suggest that if the answer is affirmative, the importance we presently assign to the ape's primitive syntax will greatly diminish. The criteria we use in deciding whether other systems resemble our own are not exclusively structural. If, when we arrived at the laboratory, an ape greeted us with "Good morning. What's for breakfast?" we would be inclined to overlook the absence of the embedded sentence. An analogy could be drawn to our evaluation of a creature we encountered on the moon. If, as we approached, it were to read to us from an official-looking document, "As the delegate of . . . I hereby welcome . . . ," we would be far less deeply persuaded of its likeness to ourselves than if it were to say, "Hey, where did you get that suit with all those shiny buttons?" Unfortunately, not all the nonstructural criteria we use to evaluate the likeness of other minds to our own are entirely decipherable, but the ability of a language to produce and express emotion is at least partially so.

We could launch the study of language and emotion by starting with nonverbal social gestures. Gestures of this kind—threats, invitations, appeasements—are major sources of emotion. Just as one kind of glance can cause an individual's face to flush with anticipation, so can another kind send him fleeing, a cold arc of fear constricting his chest. If we first established the emotion that can be controlled by gestures of this kind, we could then ask what portion of this emotion can be duplicated by linguistic means. Are there sentences that can substitute for a frown, a raised fist, a smile, an extruded tongue? We must not neglect the opposite case, of course, for there is no more reason to expect a simple equivalence in one direction than in the other. For example, we may find that no unit of language will perfectly reproduce the effect of a smile, but also that no smile or combination of nonverbal gestures will perfectly reproduce the effect of a poem.

How susceptible is the chimpanzee to the control of social gestures? A recent experiment (Woodruff and Premack 1979), though not immediately concerned with emotion but with questions of lying and deceit, will provide information relevant to that question. The basic situation was one in which the animals knew where food was hidden but could not reach it themselves; they could obtain it only by "informing" a trainer of its location. The trainers were in the opposite bind. They could move freely but did not know where the food was hidden. It was necessary for the ape to "tell" them where to go. The trainers walked from one hiding place to another, watching the animals for signs—glances, freezing, rocking—that would give away the location of the food. When a kind trainer guessed correctly and found the food, he gave it to the animal. The unkind trainer kept it for himself and gloated over it.

That is background. To appreciate how forcefully social gestures can control chimpanzees, we must turn the experiment around, putting the animals in the trainers' role, and vice versa. With this reversal of roles, the animals no longer know where the food is and must rely on the trainers to inform them. The trainers obliged the animals, pointing to one container or another—naturally, the kind trainer to the one with food, the unkind trainer to the one without food.

The pointing of the trainers exerted a remarkable control over the animals. From the beginning the animals readily followed the pointing of the kind trainer. But they also succumbed to the pointing of the unkind trainer. Only after many trials did two of the four animals overcome the deceitful gesture and take the container *not* pointed to. Two others never reached this stage. The best they could do was delay long enough to meet a time criterion, which led to our removing the unkind trainer and thus eliminating his falsely pointing arm. The animals were then free to pick the container they knew all along had the food.

Unfortunately we did not complete the experiment by substituting for the pointing arms of the kind and unkind trainers two arrows, red for truth and green for falsehood. Would it take a dozen trials for the animals to solve this cognitively elementary problem, that is, to discriminate red, pointing to the food, from green, pointing to the empty container? Or perhaps it would take a bit longer, though nothing like the several hundred trials it took them to overcome the control of the deceiving arm.

As a social gesture, the pointing arm exerted a great force, while an arrow, we may guess, would have only the power of information and exert little force. Where on this continuum would language fall? If we were to substitute for the pointing arm not the arrows but, for instance, "take the red can" or "take the green can," written in the plastic words, would the force of the verbal commands be like that of the arrow or the arm? Would the words exert the emotional force of the social gesture or have only the informational force of the arrows?

Human language can exert the force of social gestures, not in all contexts, of course, but in some. Can we find contexts in which the plastic words do the same? I raise the question to identify yet another criterion for the evaluation of language competence. Language is not only syntax, semantics, or the presuppositional system of standard pragmatics. It also has the power of social control, a power that human language derives from its connections with the human social-emotional system. Apes too have a social-emotional system: they form protracted attachments, fight with a fury, console and appease with touches. But can they appease and be appeased with words, taunt and be taunted with words? Shall we ever hear from the ape a piece of trumpery comparable to the human one "but plastic words will never hurt me"?

Though we have not yet induced emotion in apes through the use of plastic words, we have several cases of the converse, of apes expressing emotion using the plastic words. The cases are all minor, even simple, but their very simplicity dramatizes the complexity of the connections between emotion and language in the human (see William Labov, unpublished manuscript, for a recent attempt at deciphering that complexity).

Our example of emotional expression concerns Sarah's reaction to "sentences" directing her to give something to another individual. Sarah preferred writing "Mary give Sarah apple" to receiving "Sarah give Mary apple," a type of message she never produced herself. When presented with such a "sentence," she made several responses, the majority nonlinguistic. For example, she removed the sentence from the board (gently, as a rule, though she sometimes swept the words off brusquely). She had one reaction we could call "linguistic." She left "Sarah give Mary apple" on the board and, rather than carrying out the request, vigorously pressed her name—the plastic word for Sarah—into each of the pieces of apple on her work table (Premack 1976).

She visibly combined emotion with the use of her plastic word. How exactly is the emotion connected to the word? It is clearly not a syntactic connection, for there is little syntax in the single word, nor is it even semantic. "Sarah" is not a pejorative word, at least not when used by the animal so named.

The word and emotion are connected by three factors, all of which lie outside language proper: (1) locus: the apes normally apply their plastic words to the writing board, not to objects like apples; (2) intensity: the word was "stamped" forcefully into the pieces of apple; (3) repetition: the forceful action was repeated. Except perhaps for the first one, these factors are nonverbal and indicate the presence of emotion. Their appearance in connection with the plastic word recalls the shouting and repetition of speech.

In the ape, the connection between emotion and words appears to be of the most primitive kind. The chimpanzee is not another kind of poet, different only in that its poems do not contain embedded sentences. Contrary to the possibilities we contemplated earlier, we find no disparity among the several criteria that can be used to evaluate the ape's language competence. The verbal expression of emotion, like syntax and semantics, appears to be primitive in the ape.

5

Missing Linguistic Links

Several years ago, when examining what he took to be the protocol of the chimpanzee Washoe, David McNeil (1974) thought he discovered a simple rule holding for the whole protocol. The party addressed always preceded the party doing the adressing. For instance, in "Roger Washoe tickle," presumably a request for Roger to tickle Washoe, "Roger," the addressee, precedes "Washoe," the addresser. Likewise, in "Give you Washoe banana," "You give Washoe banana," "You banana give Washoe," "you," the addressee, consistently precedes "Washoe," the addresser. Unfortunately, McNeil's clever proposal must be seen as holding for a hypothetical protocol. There is no actual Washoe protocol since the Gardners evidently did not record the order of Washoe's signs so much as merely attempt to preserve their meaning or sense (Gardner and Gardner 1971). For our purposes, however, a hypothetical protocol is as good as a real one. We are not interested in the protocol but in McNeil's idea.

The interest of the idea lies in the example it provides of an intermediate language. As we are all painfully aware, nature provides no intermediate language, nothing between the lowly call system and the towering human language. McNeil's proposal, a single semantic rule mapping directly onto word order, is a possible version of an intermediate system. As such, it will illustrate nicely certain peculiarities that may apply to all intermediate systems. For instance, speakers of McNeil's system have names for all kinds of items to which the rule does *not* apply, such as names for objects ("banana"), actions ("tickle"), and properties ("red"). Whereas words that refer to the addressee and addresser come under the governance of the rule, and therefore observe word order, words that don't refer to either addresser or addressee (but name objects, actions, etc.) are not bound by the rule and should drift freely in the sentence. In addition, the individual could produce sentences having nothing to do with addressee-addresser relations: "I love Kitty," "Apples are red," "Where is Bob?" But if so, "sentences" of this kind would observe no word order at all since there is no rule that applies to them.

If this strikes you as peculiar, it can only be because human language is peculiar. All parts of the human lexicon are under the control of syntax. We do not have classes of words that are bound by rules and other classes that are not. Nor do we have topics for which there is grammatical governance (thus sentences that are well formed) and topics for which there is as yet no grammatical governance (thus sentences that are not well formed). Perhaps human language represents a late stage in the development of language; in earlier systems, rules for sentence formation may have applied only to some words and/or some topics.

The notion of a language based on "case" rather than syntax, a semantic language, has been popular for some time, more as an ontogenetic possibility, however, than as a phylogenetic one. The first or early language of the child is often seen as being of this kind, based on such categories as agent and recipient rather than on noun phrase, verb phrase, and the like. In this section, I shall deal with the general topic of missing linguistic links and with the possibility of a semantic language in the chimpanzee as a specific case of this kind. McNeil urged the credibility of his putative rule on the grounds that the chimpanzee is more advanced in social relations than in physical ones: therefore, Washoe induced a rule concerning the addresser/addressee distinction rather than one concerning physical relations. In fact, this is a dubious characterization of the chimpanzee. The animal's manipulations of the physical and social world are quite comparable; there is no evidence for a cleavage of the kind that McNeil proposed. But this need not deny the animal a semantic conceptual structure. Semantic concepts are obviously based as much on physical relations as on social ones.

How well prepared is the chimpanzee in the semantic domain and how does its preparation compare with that of the young child? We can broaden our inquiry by considering a recent account of what psycholinguists take to be the child's competence, not only in the semantic domain but in language in general. A proposal by Gleitman and Wanner (1983), acknowledging as it does earlier work by Bloom, Slobin, Bowerman, and others, may come as close as one can these days to a consensual view of the initial linguistic state of the child, that is, to the innate dispositions that enable the child to acquire language.

Gleitman and Wanner begin their account by granting the child devices that enable it to cope with a vocal language. Since words and phrases are embedded in the speech stream, rather than being given directly to the child, they equip the child with detectors for stressed elements (words) and intonation patterns (phrases). Does the ape have comparable detectors for its species-specific calls? A similar question is raised by the recent report from Mehler et al. (1981) which shows that the human infant reacts differently to sounds that do and do not have a syllabic structure. Is this contrast specific to speech or yet another acoustic distinction that would be recognized by all nonhuman species having inner ear structures resembling our own? Of course, if the ape did not have detectors of this kind, there would be no effect on its ability to acquire the artificial plastic language. Words in the case of the plastic language consist of objects not of acoustic events, and what would benefit the individual in that case would not be a stressed-element detector but the concept of object (a concept there is little doubt that the ape must have). Moreover, there should be no problem in the identification of phrases in the plastic language; the constituents of a complex string such as "red on green if then Sarah take apple" were always separated.

The second device with which Gleitman and Wanner endow the child is one enabling him to establish a correspondence between his conceptual structure and language. The child is disposed to treat separate words as separate concepts. In effect, they equip the child with a predicate calculus and then propose that the child regards each word as being either a predicate, an argument, or a logical term. What the child does not do is regard individual words as being both a predicate and an argument, both an argument and a logical term, etc.

Since I had no basis for granting comparable assumptions to the chimpanzee, I attempted instead to train the animal in a way that would optimize the development of a one-to-one correspondence between words and concepts. I arranged external situations that could be described by suitable concatenations of predicates, arguments, and sometimes logical terms and then introduced a plastic word for each of the terms in the description, one at a time. "The string [of plastic words] always [had] one incomplete slot, marked by an interrogative particle. . . . When the new word was the [predicate] both arguments were already known. . . . Conversely, when the new word was one of the arguments, the [predicate] and other arguments were known" (Premack 1983). In brief, the mapping between words and concepts could be achieved in either of two ways: by "inventing a creature" whose innate disposition would assure the mapping (which is what Gleitman and Wanner assume the child to be) and/or by inventing a procedure which, if applied to any creature that is capable of learning, would map any knowable concept onto any recognizable word.

How do children interpret the world? Relying on Lois Bloom's rich description of the child's spontaneous speech, Gleitman and Wanner conclude:

From the earliest two-word utterances, the ordering of the component words interpreted against their context of use suggests that they are conceived as playing certain thematic roles, such as *agent, instrument* and the like, within a predicate-argument (propositional) structure. . . . There seems to be little doubt that the child approaches language learning equipped with a propositional interpretation of the scenes and events in the world around him (1983, p. 14).

Can we make similar claims for the ape? The evidence for these claims in the child comes principally from the rich interpretation that has been made of the child's spontaneous speech (e.g., Bloom 1973). The evidence in the ape could not come from spontaneous speech but from such sources as the analysis the ape makes of action.

Action is, after all, the source of all semantic distinctions— agent, object, patient, instrument, and all the rest. People act, to begin with, in the real world, not in sentences. They act on objects, on one another, with and without instruments, in dyads and triads, with and without reciprocation, and so on. To appreciate the distinctions of a case grammar and to use them in organizing one's language one must first of all be able to recognize these distinctions in action itself. Can the chimpanzee do that?

We have shown, in an extended series of tests, that the chimpanzee can recognize arbitrary visual illustrations of the idea of action. Simple physical actions can be represented by a three-element sequence consisting of an object in its initial condition, an instrument, and the object in its transformed or terminal condition. For example, cutting can be illustrated by an apple, a knife, a cut apple; wetting by a dry sponge, container of water, a wet sponge; marking by blank paper, a writing instrument, marked paper. When given representations of this kind that were incomplete in either the instrument or the transformed object, language-trained chimpanzees consistently chose alternatives that properly completed the representations (Premack 1976, p. 251; 1983).

In a still more direct attack on the chimpanzee's grasp of basic semantic concepts, we showed Sarah videotapes of simple actions—Bill cutting an orange, John marking paper with a pencil, Henry washing an apple with water—and required her to identify the different components of the action. She was given three different markers, which were sticky pieces of paper varying in color, shape, and size that adhered to the television monitor, and was trained to place them on different parts of the scene. One marker was to go on the agent of the action (Bill, John, Henry), another on the object of the action (orange, paper, apple), and a third on the instrument of the action (knife, pencil, water). After reaching criterion on the three training tapes, Sarah was given a transfer test in which all of her responses were approved. The transfer tests were uniquely demanding, for the scenes were not merely new, but also decidedly more complex than those used in training. Where the training scenes had been simple—one person acting on one object with one instrument—the transfer scenes were complex—two objects, only one of which was acted on; two instruments, only one of which was used; and two persons, only one of whom carried out the action. The other individual was engaged in some scenes as an observer of the action of the first person and in other scenes as the recipient of the action (e.g., Bill brushed Bob's hair).

The results were both impressive and, in the long run, somewhat disappointing. Sarah passed the transfer tests; her use of all three markers was above chance though her accuracy was poor. She had her greatest success with the agent marker (85 percent correct overall) and was able to distinguish the individual who conducted the action from one who either observed it or was its recipient. She was only moderately successful with the object marker (67 percent correct overall) and still less successful with the instrument marker (62 percent correct overall).

We attempted to improve her accuracy by training her on the transfer series; we corrected her errors, where earlier we had approved all her responses. The attempt did not simply fail, it led to yet another of those surprises of which Sarah seems to have an infinite supply. She began to put all three markers on the blank part of the screen, where there was neither agent, object, nor instrument. Although this response was never seen in either the original training or in the transfer series, by the third session of our attempted retraining it had become her most common response. The response could be seen as her way of refusing to commit herself; in any case, it so dominated the lesson that further training was pointless (Premack and Woodruff, unpublished data). That outcomes of this kind are not uncommon with the sophisticated adult chimpanzee does not make them any easier to interpret.

I take her basic success on the initial transfer series, though below her usual quality, to indicate an ability to draw the semantic distinctions in question. Her refusal to improve or perfect this ability with further training indicates that the task is a demanding one (in retrospect, we probably should have dropped one of the categories, either object or instrument, and settled for a two-way rather than a three-way distinction). Perhaps the reader should bear in mind that four-year-old children do not pass the transfer tests given Sarah. When trained and tested as Sarah was, they do not define the markers as agent, object, and instrument of the action, but draw a much simpler distinction, animate/inanimate (or perhaps person/nonperson). That is, they reserve the would-be *agent marker* for people, but without regard for whether the person is an actor, observer, or recipient of the action. Similarly, they reserve the would-be *object* and *instrument markers* for nonpersons, again without regard for whether the object or instrument is in actual use or is simply present. These are the results Kim Dolgin obtained when she applied Sarah's test procedure to young children. With the children, Dolgin took a further step that could not be taken with Sarah. The four-year-old children were told, while viewing the training examples, the meaning of agent, object, and instrument. They then passed the transfer tests at a high level of accuracy. College sophomores, in contrast, do not need verbal definitions. For them, the nonverbal training—only partly successful with Sarah—was entirely successful (Dolgin 1981).

How shall we reconcile Sarah's (even) partial success on the semantic concepts with two other aspects of chimpanzee behavior: the ape's total absence of a natural language and the animal's limited success in acquiring a simplified language in the laboratory? Given the ape's ability to distinguish agent, recipient, and instrument, one might suppose that the feral chimpanzee would have a natural language; specifically, a semantic grammar, properly simplified, in which the semantic role of the word mapped directly onto, say, the surface ordering of the string. One might also suppose that the ape could readily be taught such a language in the laboratory. But neither of these conditions holds.

Notice that one cannot object to the possibility of a natural semantic language on the grounds that case grammars "won't work." Case grammars evidently will not work for human language because of its complex mapping rules. In English we find "Sarah is easy to please" and "Sarah is eager to please," where the semantic role of "Sarah" varies while its sentential position does not. Conversely, in "Mary gave Sarah apple" and "Sarah received apple from Mary" the semantic role of "Sarah" does not vary despite its variation in sentential position. But while this kind of complexity is evidently a characteristic of all human language, it is not a necessary or integral characteristic of language.

We might define language as a discursive representational system that can be used to carry out certain functions; which of them are actually carried out will vary with the general abilities of the individual who knows the language. Principal among these functions are reference and truth claims. Truth claims, for example, depend on two conditions: descriptions and the ability to make what amount to same/different judgments about the relation between the description and the condition described. We hardly need complex mapping rules for descriptions; even a finite state grammar would do. And the chimpanzee is capable of making the necessary same/different judgments. For instance, when Sarah was shown a red card on a green one and asked "Is red on green?" ("? red on green"), she reliably replaced the interrogative particle with the appropriate "yes" or "no." Complex mapping rules, of the kind that make case grammars inadequate for human language, are not needed to carry out such basic language functions as truth claims; one wonders if there are any functions of language for which they are needed.

In a very real sense, the two principal peculiarities of human language are an evolutionary embarrassment. It is not easy to picture the scenarios that would confer selective fitness on, specifically, syntactic classes and structure-dependent rules. While linguists advise us that these are formal properties without which human language cannot be modeled, it is not at all clear what functional properties of language are served specifically by these formal properties. Perhaps recursiveness is such a property; it may depend on syntactic classes. Let us pretend that it does: I, at least, do not see how to realize recursiveness without syntactic classes. These classes afford the kind of abstract representation in which the rewrite rules, needed for recursiveness, can be easily realized. But if this is correct, even in the weak sense that syntactic classes provide an economical or simple access to recursiveness, the peculiarities of human language would remain no less an evolutionary embarrassment.

I challenge the reader to reconstruct the scenario that would confer selective fitness on recursiveness. Language evolved, it is conjectured, at a time when humans or protohumans were hunting mastodons. Having language would be a benefit to them. They could do social planning, discuss strategies together, lay plans for specific contingencies. Now the alleged advantage of recursiveness is not simply unlimited sentences but, even more perhaps, the compacting of information. Would it be a great advantage for one of our ancestors, squatting alongside the embers, to be able to remark: "Beware of the short beast whose front hoof Bob cracked when, having forgotten his own spear back at camp, he got in a glancing blow with the dull spear he borrowed from Jack"?

Human language is an embarrassment for evolutionary theory because it is vastly more powerful than one can account for in terms of selective fitness. A semantic language with simple mapping rules, of a kind one might suppose the chimpanzee would have, appears to confer all the advantages one normally associates with discussions of mastodon hunting or the like. For discussions of that kind, syntactic classes, structure-dependent rules, recursion, and the rest are overly powerful devices, absurdly so. Moreover, the neurological basis of these formal properties could not be without cost.

We have two ways in which to alleviate the embarrassment to evolutionary theory of a language more powerful than it can explain. First, we could maintain that there were hominids who had simple languages, but they did not survive. Their progeny, who also did not survive, had somewhat more complex languages, and so on; present human language being the last of a series of progressively more complex and powerful languages. How susceptible to disconfirmation is this proposal? Although Phil Lieberman (1973) and his associates have cleverly proposed models of speech perception that span thousands of years — enabling the testing of hypotheses about extremely remote events — few evolutionary hypotheses enjoy this degree of testability. Many of them, given their inaccessibility to disconfirmation, seem more like just-so stories than scientific hypotheses, and I am not sure that this does not apply in the present case. There is also the stark absence of natural language in contemporary pongids, an absence made the more puzzling by what we now know of the chimpanzee's ability to make at least some semantic distinctions. Second, we could adopt a liberated view of evolution, treating language, and all other hard-to-explain cases, not as traits that evolved in direct response to selective advantage but as coincidental by-products of traits or systems that did so evolve. This seems dangerously close to a cop-out. To be sure, believers in evolutionary theory will not be disturbed by this liberated view; but those who find the data of evolution more convincing than the theories are not likely to be appeased by such a view.

In a challenging recent book, Lieberman (1985) argues that language and cognition arose essentially from walking and breathing. Neural mechanisms that now structure language and cognition were preadapted to control motor behavior, or as he puts it, "The rules of syntax derive from a generalization of neural mechanisms that gradually evolved in the motor cortex to facilitate the automatization of motor activity" (p. 67). The changes that resulted in the specialized mechanisms of human language are in no way unique; the same process of Darwinian selection accounts for the evolution of homologous mechanisms in other animals. Again, it is better said by Lieberman:

Human language . . . is different from the communication systems of other animals in the same sense that the communication system of a dog differs from that of a frog. It is more complex . . . and involves different . . . mechanisms. [But] these mechanisms are related in a biological and evolutionary sense (p. 2).

Lieberman would agree with Bertrand Russell (1940), who observed that speaking is no less a motor activity than is jumping, the two differing only in that one has meaning. But, unlike Russell, Lieberman seeks to reunite the two categories of action, claiming in effect that saying "frog," "there's a frog," "frogs are green," and all the rest ultimately evolved from the jumping of the frog.

The strongest evidence for Lieberman's striking claim would lie in a demonstration of the formal parallel between the syntax of the two kinds of motor activity, speech and nonspeech. The claim of such parallels is not new. Indeed, a common shibboleth begins by verbally wagging its finger at us—"language is *not* the only rule-governed behavior!"—and ends by promising us grammars for the nonverbal cases—play (Reynolds 1972) and toolmaking (Lieberman 1975) being perennial favorites. Unfortunately, however, as the years have passed, grammars for nonverbal cases have proved to be neither finite state nor phrase structure but promissory. Lieberman, an early advocate of the shibboleth, no longer mentions toolmaking or play but offers instead a finite-state model for drinking a glass of water. The rules of his grammar consist of, for example, "extend arm toward tumbler," "close hand on tumbler," "drink from tumbler." The absence of any parallel between this grammar and that of human language hardly needs further comment.

Those writing grammars for nonverbal behavior encounter two kinds of problems, one serious, the other merely fatal. The lack of self-evident units constitutes the serious problem. Since nonverbal sequences are not predivided into units (while sentences come divided into words), such units as are typically proposed— "drink from tumbler," "extend arm toward tumbler"—have an arbitrary character. Why these units rather than indefinitely many others?

But this need not be an insuperable problem. The units of nonverbal sequences can be uncovered by a simple procedure proposed some years ago (Premack 1976, p. 54). In effect, we ask the individual (whose motor sequences we are studying) "to tell" where the "joints" or immediate constituents in his behavior are. We do so by recording (visual, auditory) his motor sequences, "cutting" the sequences into pieces, and then using the pieces as contingent events in a reinforcement paradigm. For example, by pressing a bar the individual can see (hear, touch) himself make a social gesture, utter a call, operate on the inanimate environment, or the like. Not all portions of the call, social gesture, and so on will be equally reinforcing. Some portions will, I suggest, *maximize the reinforcement function*, and those portions that are maximizing can be regarded as nonarbitrary units of nonverbal sequences. But if this approach should fail, then surely some other approach will succeed. The units are not the critical problem in writing grammars for nonverbal behavior.

The fundamental problem has to do with the categories in terms of which the rules are to be formulated. Lieberman does not deal directly with this problem but presents examples of rules; his examples, as indicated above, serve only to illustrate the gravity of the problem. "Pick up," "drink," "tumbler," some of the categories he uses, could not differ more radically from "noun phrase," "verb phrase," "determiner"—the categories of human syntax. Syntactic categories are defined not on perceptual and/or functional grounds, but solely by the role they play in the rules of the syntax; whereas Lieberman's categories are defined not by the role they play in the rules, but solely on perceptual and/or functional grounds.

Although linguists disagree on many issues, as do most scientists, they are virtually of one mind as to the necessity for using formal categories in formulating the rules of human language. Those who dissent (claiming either that semantic or pragmatic categories will suffice) are a distinct minority. Consider, for example, the grammars of Chomsky (1965) and Bresnan (1978) and an ATN grammar (e.g., Wanner and Maratsos 1978), grammars that differ widely. Despite their differences, they all show the same commitment to the necessity of formal categories: noun phrase and verb phrase appear in each.

To demonstrate a serious parallel between the syntax of language and that of nonverbal motor behavior, Lieberman must show at least one of two conditions. Either (1) that grammars for human language can be written without formal categories or (2) that there are formal categories for nonverbal behavior. If he fails, we must conclude that language and nonlanguage differ fundamentally, leaving the emergence of one from the other as much a mystery as it ever was.

The recent demonstration of conditioning in Aplysia (Carews, Walters, and Kandel 1981) has led Lieberman to conclude that mollusks think and have cognition. While the demonstration of conditioning in this simple invertebrate is of great interest, conditioning is exactly the kind of mechanism that will *not* account for cognition. That mollusks think, as Lieberman proposes, is hard to say, as thinking is not a technical term. Whether they engage in cognition may be easier to decide. We have a better chance of restricting "cognition" to a technical meaning, for example, the construction of mental representations on which one makes computations.

In the conditioning process, one event A is associated with another event B through temporal and/or spatial contiguity, a mechanism that, as Dickinson (1980) suggests, may be the precursor of the cause-effect relations found later in the vertebrate. It is possible that this simple mechanism was among the first to have been added to creatures in which there was "genotypic change over generations" but as yet no "phenotypic change within the individual." Experience, we might say, was invented with conditioning, where by "experience" we mean not simply reaction to the world (necessarily present from the start) but, far more important, reaction that led to a more or less permanent change. However, with this (perhaps) earliest form of experience—of phenotypic rather than genotypic change—we are still far from cognition, that is, far from the construction of mental models of the world and computing on those models.

Moreover, the complex behavioral mechanisms for which insects and spiders are renowned—for example, the bee's adjustment of the direction indicated in its dance to the rotation of the earth, the spider's adjustment of the thickness of its strand to weights attached to its back—are not ipso facto evidence of cognition. It would be desirable to know whether experience affects the accuracy of these adjustments, but developmental psychology has yet to reach the invertebrate. In the meantime, we guess (safely) that these adjustments are not produced by computations on mental representations. Their complexity is our clue—bees are not geometers, nor spiders engineers! Nor are these adjustments learned. They are the output of hard-wired components about which we presently know far too little.

The human's hard-wired components are an equal mystery. An association between complexity (on the one hand) and performance that is neither learned nor computed (on the other) is not unique to the insect. The syntax of human language may well depend on hard-wired components (Chomsky 1980). The most complex achievements of all species probably depend heavily on hard-wired components. Mollusks, spiders, insects—invertebrates generally—differ from humans not in their lack of hard-wired components but in their lack of cognition. Griffin's phrase "cognitive ethology" (1976), when applied to invertebrates, appears to be a colorful misnomer, rather like "equatorial Norway" or the "nautical jungle."

Vertebrates associate events not only on the basis of contiguity in space or time, but also on the basis of physical resemblance. Such species categorize or place "like" items together, *A* with *A*, *B* with *B*, and so on. When the sorting mechanism is strong (as it is especially in children and to a lesser extent in apes), their performance is spontaneous; when the mechanism is weak (as it is in monkeys, even weaker in pigeons), the performance comes only after explicit and extensive training. Invertebrates, presumably, could not be trained to demonstrate their comprehension of a rule instantiating physical similarity. Moreover, this use of physical similarity is the merest departure from the putting together of items associated through contiguity in time and/or place—that is, conditioning.

At another level, species place like things together, but the meaning of "like" has now deepened. These species match not only *A* with *A* but also *AA* with *BB* (rather than *CD*) and *CD* with *EF* (rather than *BB*). Physical resemblance "evolves" into conceptual equivalence. Cognition may enter at this point. Or, stating the issue differently, the *capacity* for computing conceptual equivalence may indicate abstract mental representation and be, therefore, a good litmus test for cognition (Premack 1983).

Everything discussed so far is utterly preliminary to that which is intriguing about human intelligence. There has been no recourse to, say, Shakespeare, Beethoven, or Buddha, no appeal to the company of geniuses to distinguish mollusk from human. But poetry, music, and religion are a nontrivial part of humans; no theory of intelligence has the slightest chance of being even partly complete without the explication of these forms. The hardest part of the explication will lie, no doubt, in identifying the hard-wired components that participate in these activities. It is in the human that hard-wiring, learning, and cognition combine in their most formidable and perplexing ways.

There are evolutionary theorists whose positions are preferable to the gradualism or seamless continuity of Lieberman's.

"All species are unique," Dobzhansky once remarked, "but humans are uniquest" (1955, p. 12). This distinguished evolutionist, with his jibe, has spared us the idle query, "Are humans unique?" and directed us to the proper query, "What is the nature of the self-evident human uniqueness?"

The continuity that Lieberman finds among all species comes from peering through a telescope with an exceptional focal length. Human and mollusk, viewed at this distance, blend into the same creature. Of course, the classic question in any attempt at synthesis is the amount of detail that can be rubbed off the individual pieces (so that they may join and reveal a pattern) without destroying their integrity. One cannot read Lieberman's attempt at synthesis without admiring the boldness. But the trick is to solve the puzzle without bending or defacing the pieces.

Recursion

Chomsky has made a specific proposal concerning the evolution of human language based on a mutation (not, as in Lieberman's case, on normal Darwinian selection). He calls our attention

to the curious fact that the number concept—i.e., the understanding that one can add one indefinitely—appears in the species that has a language based on discrete infinity.... A very simple mutation may have changed a species with a conceptual system based on standard thematic relations . . . into a species with something like human language: namely, a mutation that permitted recursion and embedding, and thus gave rise to the notion of discrete infinity (providing the number concept automatically . . .) (personal communication 1984).

Here we have Chomsky's version of what we now recognize as the standard argument: humans, like other intelligent species, had "a conceptual system based on standard thematic relations"; but intelligence alone does not make for human language—a special factor is needed. This time the special factor is a mutation making possible both recursion and embedding, and, at the same time, human quantificational ability.

Do humans really have a monopoly on recursion, as Chomsky's proposal suggests? In communication and judgment of number, nonhuman species, as far as we know, do nothing that would warrant invoking recursive rules. But there are other fields of endeavor in which we might find evidence of this kind, for recursion is by no means tied to any specific field.

A nice example of a recursive procedure (for which I'm indebted to Professor Herbert Wilf, University of Pennsylvania Math Department) is one that could be used to find the heaviest object in a set of objects all of which look alike. Professor Wilf's example is not only exquisitely simple, it has the additional merit of illustrating iteration as well as recursion, and thus of contrasting the two. Suppose an individual were given a number of visually identical boxes and asked to find the heaviest one. He starts by picking up one box in each hand, hefting or comparing them, and then discarding the lighter one. Next he picks up a third box, compares it with the one he kept from the first comparison, and once again discards the lighter one. He repeats this procedure, taking care to keep the discards in a separate pile, until he exhausts the supply of boxes. This is not a recursive procedure but a merely iterative one. The same rule, compare two boxes and retain the heavier one, is applied repeatedly until the boxes are exhausted.

A simple change will make the procedure recursive. First, the individual divides the boxes into two subsets. He compares the members of one subset until he finds the heaviest box and then puts that box aside; he repeats the procedure with the second subset and puts that box aside. Then he compares the heaviest box from each subset, keeping the heavier of the two. The procedure is recursive, as the first one was not, because the same rule was used on two levels—first in selecting the appropriate member from each subset and then in choosing between the selections from the two subsets. The simplicity of the case is such that we would do well to try it with both apes and children.

A problem that has been tried with chimpanzees is Emile Menzle's version of the so-called traveling salesman problem (1973). Menzle hid pieces of fruit in a field while the animals watched and then released the animals into the field to recover the fruit. The animals not only found most of the fruit, but, more importantly, they also took an economical path in doing so, seldom retracing their steps as they went from one piece to another. Their success was the more remarkable because, as the reader will observe, the fruit was not visible and the animal was connecting locations in memory. Unfortunately, however, the paths taken by the animals could be generated by a simple iterative procedure, by applying the so-called "nearest neighbor rule" over and over; that is, always go to the fruit closest to the one where you are. If this is what the chimpanzees did, then their success in recovering the fruit leaves us where we were, empty handed, still without evidence of recursion in a nonhuman species.

From Ape to Child?

Can we regard the chimpanzee that has been exposed to language training as a test of the Gleitman-Wanner model? If at first this strikes the reader as a bizarre proposal, he should need no more than a moment's reflection to see that the proposal is actually quite reasonable. Moreover, he should also see that if the model is correct, the chimpanzee should acquire language. The basis for the prediction is straightforward: either the dispositions that are assumed for the child can also be assumed for the ape, or else we can substitute for the dispositions, in effect replacing internal conditions with external ones. For instance, although the ape's conceptual structure must be far weaker than the child's, surely the ape must have such a structure. Whatever we may decide to make of the vexed concept "concept"—abstract sorting device or the like—the problems we have in assuming such a device for the ape can be no greater than they are for the child. In addition, the ape resembles the child in "reading" the world in terms of semantic-relational thematic roles such as agent, recipient, instrument. On the other hand, there are dispositions in the child we need not invoke in the ape, for example, stressed element and intonation detectors as well as the disposition to map one concept onto one word. In these cases, as we saw earlier, we can replace the child's putative disposition with an external condition—stressed element detector with cut pieces of plastic in the one case and one-to-one mapping with a training program in the other. In brief, if Gleitman and Wanner have accurately enumerated the dispositions enabling the child to acquire language, we have good reason to believe that, with proper training, we should be able to turn an ape into a child. Not the brightest child, of course, but nonetheless a child.

In fact, we cannot turn the ape into any kind of child, bright or otherwise. There are, to be sure, people who believe otherwise. But for the most part these are people who have never seen an ape (let alone tried to talk to a "talking" one), people whose experience is confined to commercial videotapes and who cannot be good observers in the first place. To my consternation, two of my most able friends are included in this group. They *are* good observers, so we must seek explanation elsewhere. We do not have far to look: they share an adamant, even truculent, determination to brook no suggestion of discontinuity between human and animal (for reasons that are profoundly different, though we need not go into that here). They are redeemable, however: neither of them has ever seen a "talking" ape.

That apes cannot be turned into children suggests that the Gleitman-Wanner account of the child is incomplete. The model may stand a good chance of being correct in the dispositions that it identifies, but evidently it has left out some important ones, for, in a sense, they must bear the burden of explaining the irrefragable difference we find between child and ape.

The two principal factors Gleitman and Wanner do not discuss in the context of the young child are syntactic categories (which they leave for the older child) and inductive processes, those processes by which either semantic-relational or syntactic categories are turned into the kinds of rules needed for a grammar. Given the degree to which ape intelligence has been celebrated, we might suppose that data confirming the ape's inductive capacity were already at hand. In fact, such data are in short supply. The problem solving that Köhler showed over fifty years ago (1925) and the reasoning that we have demonstrated more recently (McClure et al., in preparation) do not, unfortunately, provide a good basis for evaluating the ape's ability to induce rules. Our reasoning studies do go beyond Köhler's problem-solving studies in that they explicitly require inference, the filling in of information that is not given perceptually; but they make no more specific contribution to rule induction or theory construction than do the earlier studies of problem solving. Not until we have better models of reasoning can we compare the possible use of rules or other devices that may be involved in problem solving with the induction of rules or construction of theories that appear to be required in the formation of a grammar.

Certainly we do not find in the ape anything remotely comparable to the reorganization of data and the resulting empowered rules that Bowerman (1983) finds in the slightly older child's development of language; to the spontaneous development of derivational morphological systems that Newport (1983) has spelled out in the signing child; or to the metacognitive tasks that Karmiloff-Smith (1979) has demonstrated in the child (and proposed as cognitive analogues of grammatical rule development in the child). Hence we cannot dismiss, at this time, the possibility that the ape's lack of language, both natural and laboratory, reflects a basic inductive weakness.

The claim that language does not depend on general intelligence needs to be reexamined. It is based on two errors. The first is the supposition that the two normally opposed views— those of general intelligence and a unique linguistic factor— are mutually exclusive and therefore properly contrasted. The second is a parochial view of intelligence, which is based incorrectly on comparisons within rather than between species.

If a linguistic factor were to be added to a species whose intelligence was below a certain level, it would have, as I already suggested, no practical effect. But let us make the argument more specific. Suppose the linguistic factor we added consisted specifically of syntactic categories. These are, in fact, excellent candidates for the job because, evidently, human grammar cannot be modeled without them and because there is a growing consensus among psycholinguists that syntax cannot be derived from semantics. No metamorphosis has been demonstrated for turning semantic caterpillars into syntactic butterflies: "agent," "recipient," and the like, no matter how abstractly construed, will not turn into "noun phrase," "verb phrase," etc. Now suppose we add syntactic categories to the ape—actually discover their neurological basis and, by delicate brain surgery, implant them in the ape. The surgery could fail, though perfectly executed, because the ape is not smart enough, where "smart" now means having the inductive capacity to frame grammatical rules with the categories in question. In fact, for all we presently know, the ape may already have syntactic categories but cannot give evidence of having them because the surgery that it really needs is one that would implant an upgraded inductive capacity.

A parochial construal of intelligence, in which within-species comparisons have improperly substituted for the needed between-species comparisons, has also contributed to a sense of incompatibility between the "unique factor" and "general intelligence" views. Lenneberg, a main progenitor of this position, noted (1967) that some retarded children have language, which means that language could not depend on intelligence. But retarded children, at least those retarded children who have language, are far more intelligent than apes (the result we get in every comparison of this kind we have made). Moreover, the language found in many retarded children differs appreciably from normal human language (see, for example, Ann Fowler 1984). As Lenneberg was himself the first to observe, the retarded child's language appears to be equivalent to an earlier stage of normal human language. The rules of this earlier stage are weaker than those of adult grammar; they predate the "reorganization of data" (Bowerman 1982) that ushers in the more powerful adult rules, and they are of a kind that could be formulated by inductive capacities weaker than those needed for adult grammar. Are syntactic classes needed to model this weaker system of the retarded, or is it a semantic system? Here opinion differs, though the majority view is that the system is syntactic. Thus, the prevailing view of the retarded child's language problems speaks to intelligence per se, to a deficiency in inductive capacity rather than in syntactic categories.

On the other hand, mentioning "general intelligence" implies a central factor, comparable to Spearman's *G* (1937), as the would-be source of all problem-solving; but there is no current evidence that problem-solving has a unitary source. The ability to solve spatial problems may be unrelated to the ability to solve nonspatial analogies, and these in turn unrelated to the ability to construct human grammar. Although there are interesting similarities between the problems faced by the child in constructing a grammar and the standard problems in scientific induction (see Fodor 1966, p. 109 for a discussion of the parallels), we cannot conclude that these similarities suggest a relation between the two tasks (as Fodor 1984 would unhesitatingly point out).

If the factors that underlie the construction of human grammar do play a substantial role in the construction of scientific theory, all of us would be distinguished scientists. Indeed, the task the child accomplishes in constructing human grammar seems far more complex than that of the scientist in constructing a scientific theory. Moreover, scientific theory is the work not of the individual, but of generations of individuals, each building on the achievements of the other. The construction of human grammar is the work of a single individual. And a young one at that. The ape, whose ability at both science and language is limited, might, through brain surgery (of the kind mentioned above) realize improvement on one task without gaining on the other. If the ape's surgically constructed brain bore any resemblance to the normal human brain, this outcome would be no surprise.

Turn now to a second factor which Gleitman and Wanner deny the younger child, reserving it for the older one—syntactic categories. Agreeing with many psycholinguists, they treat the child's first language as semantic in nature. They are quick to observe, however, that this assumption, though simplifying in some ways, creates other problems. The adult ends up with a syntactic grammar, so if we start the child with a semantic grammar, we are left to explain the transition, which, as we saw earlier, is not a simple one. The whole problem can be avoided by putting syntax into the child's language from the start. As this section will show, there may be other reasons as well for starting the child out with syntax.

The drawbacks of constructing a language without syntactic building blocks can be seen in the language taught Sarah. Indeed, in analyzing Sarah's language we will see not only the problems posed by the lack of syntax, but also, more surprisingly, that these problems cannot be entirely overcome by replacing the missing syntactic categories with semantic ones.

Consider some of the sentence types Sarah was taught, each of which was tailored to serve a particular condition. For example, one sentence type described acts of *giving*, another the condition of *on*. A third was used for talking about properties instantiated by objects, and a fourth concerned same/different relations ("apple is red same red color of apple"). The rule for the description of giving was: donor, act, object, recipient (e.g., "Mary give apple Sarah," "Sarah give banana Donna." The rule for *on* was equally simple: object on top, relation, object on the bottom (e.g., "clay on plate," "red on green"). And the rule for the instantiation of properties was also simple: property, relation, instantiating object (e.g., "small size of pea," "blue color of grape").

It is essential to see that these rules are unrelated. That is, they are not framed in terms of common categories and indeed have virtually nothing in common beyond the mechanics of using word order as a mapping device. This mélange of independent rules could have been avoided, however. We could have taught Sarah a narrower language, one dealing exclusively with topics to which semantic categories apply. And, given Sarah's capacity for semantic distinctions, we might then have formulated the rules for all her sentence types from a common set of categories. Sentences like "Bill cut apple," "Sarah take grape in green dish," and "Mary insert orange" would have realized this objective. We did, to be sure, use many such sentences with Sarah, and they may have contributed to our even limited success. But we also used many others that did not concern action, including sentences dealing with the instantiation of properties, the conditional relation, same/different relations, and they may have contributed to our lack of success.

A human adult looking at Sarah's sentences would deny the necessary independence or unrelatedness of the rules that generated them. For example, in considering "Mary give apple Sarah," "red on green," and "blue color of grape," he would contend that, while only one of them deals with action, they have much in common, including that "Mary," "red," and "blue" are each the subject of their respective sentences. Our observer is, of course, entirely correct, but the distinction applies only to the human reader and not to Sarah. For "subject of the sentence" is not a distinction available to Sarah or to any other creature who has language formulated in semantic categories.

Unlike the human adult, Sarah had no set of categories with which to unify the rules of her several sentence types and would therefore have had to learn nearly every rule separately, without benefitting from having learned the others. Perhaps this will account in part for why the limited system taught Sarah did not "take off," show accelerated development at some point, the way language does in the child.

Admittedly, semantic and syntactic categories are not the only ways to unify the rules of a language; the predicate calculus is a third alternative. The applicability of the predicate-argument format to Sarah's sentences is obvious in the case of simple strings such as "Bill cut apple," but no less applicable in the case of more complex strings such as "red on green if-then Sarah take apple" (in which the conditional particle is the predicate and the two short sentences are the arguments). I was often dimly aware that Sarah's "sentences" could be analyzed in these terms, and I probably benefitted from it in making up sentences for her lessons. But was the analysis available to Sarah? Did she sense the structural parallel between, say, "Bill cut apple" and "red on green if-then Sarah take apple" and benefit from it? One suspects that the answer is negative, but we have no evidence one way or the other.

Were children to begin language in the only way possible for Sarah, without syntactic categories, they too would seem to suffer the disadvantages described for Sarah. Perhaps, however, children in the beginning do not talk about topics for which they cannot make a semantic analysis, and unlike Sarah, they are not beset by lessons in which sentences of an uncongenial kind are forced upon them. Nevertheless, sentences that adults address to children may not be limited to topics for which a semantic analysis is applicable. If only for this reason, it would be to the child's advantage to begin with syntactic categories.

Apes may lack adequate inductive or theory-constructive capacities, as well as syntactic categories, and therefore lack natural language (and may be slow to acquire artificial ones). Whatever the ape may lack in requirements for language, social communication is certainly not one. On the grounds of a compelling parallel between the structure of social action and that of the sentence, many researchers find the origin of language in social communication. Bruner expresses this widely held view when he says: "The structure of human action in infancy . . . corresponds to the structure of universal case categories. It is the infant's success in achieving joint action (or the mother's success for that matter) that virtually leads him into language" (1975, p. 6). Proponents of this view, which include many thoughtful people (Bates 1979; Greenfield and Smith 1976), do not appear to have given the animal communication literature serious consideration. If they had, they would observe that their position predicts language for every social species and is thus grossly at odds with what we actually find.

For example, the Dutch ethologist Plooij (1978), after minutely examining the communication between mother and infant chimpanzee, lays out a course of development for intentional communication in the ape that appears to parallel the human one in every major respect. First, the infant is groomed by its mother, who raises the infant's arm in doing so. Not long after, the infant approaches the mother and seeks grooming by raising its own arm. At first, however, it does this without seeking eye contact with the mother. Not long after, the infant carries out a perfect example of intentional communication. It gains the mother's gross attention by a tug perhaps, looks into her eyes for more certain or specific assurance, and only when successful in eye contact raises its arm before her. Plooij also finds that arm-raising occurs in different contexts and serves different functions in older infants and that acts of this general kind occur in combinations. Perhaps humans do possess social elements lacking in apes, but if so, the study of social communication has yet to approach the exactness that would permit identifying them. The development of chimpanzee social communication appears to approximate human development. Probably monkey development approximates that of the chimpanzee, while rodent development may bear interesting similarities to that of the monkey. Yet none of these nonhuman species have natural language, which they should if language arose from a structural parallel between sentence and social action. Indeed, if this parallel accounted for language, we should find, in every social species a language proportional in complexity to the complexity of the social communication, find, therefore, a perfect continuity of languages. We find instead not only a discontinuity between human and nonhuman, but also the lack of any degree of language among nonhumans.

Recent work on call systems has addressed that discontinuity, which George Miller summarized in his remark: "If there were prelinguistic forms of vocal communication, none of the hominids that used them have survived: there is today an enormous gap in communicative abilities between human beings and all other animals" (1983, p. 31). Earlier interpretations of call systems were too simple. Calls of the vervet monkey, for example, do not merely reflect emotional states of the speaker but are specific for different predators (Struthshaker 1967; Cheney and Seyfarth 1982). Moreover, some animal calls occur in sequences whose "meaning" changes with the order of the calls (Beer 1976). Nevertheless, this enlightened view of the call system hardly vitiates the gap between human and nonhuman communication abilities on which Miller comments. On the contrary, what remains as the most vivid feature of the animal call system is the meagerness of the evidence it provides for intermediate systems. Even in a transition from insect to primate, there is negligible growth in the size, complexity, or scope of reference of the call system. Vertebrates have more calls than invertebrates, for instance, perhaps twenty in the bee versus thirty-five in the ape (Moynihan 1970), but this hardly seems an impressive difference. The differences among vertebrates are even smaller: the call system of the ape would be hard to tell from that of even a gopher. Scant evidence indeed for intermediate systems between human and nonhuman!

On the other hand, how distinctive is the gap between human and nonhuman communicative abilities? Are there not comparable gaps in every cognitive module, in number competence, face recognition, spatial representation, and the like? Perhaps the interspecies differences in these cases are not less than they are in communicative ability. This is not an easy question to answer—there are too many untested cases—but such evidence as we have suggests the following.

Differences between the species are the smallest in what might be regarded as basic skills, skills prerequisite for solving problems common to every species. Thus, in short-term (and even intermediate-term) memory, apes, dolphins, and humans look remarkably alike (Hayes et al. 1953; Thompson and Herman 1977). Continuity may be even greater in the mental representation of space. Not just intelligent species but all vertebrates may share some basic features, for example, mental maps of space characterized by Euclidean geometry (Cheng and Gallistel 1984). In reasoning the similarities cannot be as great, even though we find, surprisingly, that the chimpanzee can do analogies (Gillan et al. 1981) as well as make inferences of a spatial kind.

Interspecies differences are greatest in skills that are not prerequisite for solving problems common to all species but are species specific. Quantitative skills, for instance, are decidedly a human specialization (Gelman and Gallistel 1978), and the gap between human and ape in these skills (Woodruff and Premack 1981) may be no less than it is in language. Of course, this is close to a circular proposal that says little more than that species can specialize and when they do, they will differ more than when they do not. Yet even this circular proposal sets the stage for the point at issue. We find the language gap deeply puzzling while at the same time we blithely accept a comparable gap in quantitative ability. One gap is tolerable, even sensible, while the other is a major evolutionary puzzle. Why?

The answer is not hard to find. We regard the problem of communication as basic, as confronting every species, but we hardly see counting or arithmetic in this light. So the conundrum is this: Why has the human become so specialized in communication?

In fact, however, communication is a poor way to characterize the human specialization and language an even poorer way. Communication is preferable to language because it at least correctly connotes that the human specialization is intensely social in nature. The specialization consists of a number of separable though interwoven dispositions (for which unfortunately we lack a single name) whose net effect is to link humans in a social unit that extends across generations, giving rise to history and tradition. A main source of this linkage is pedagogy: key factors interlocking with pedagogy are aesthetics, social attribution, and consciousness. The dovetailing of these factors produces the kind of social binding that results in the human group.

At one level, pedagogy is the disposition to control the behavior of others as one controls one's own behavior. The infant, captivated by the discovery that it can control its own body, turns into the adult, who seeks to control not only his own body but that of others as well. Could a disposition be more rapacious? Yet the pedagogic disposition is benign, rescued by the fact that the control is for the benefit of the other party. The goal of pedagogy is not self-benefit, but to bring the behavior of the other one into conformity with a set of standards. The standards may appear to concern efficiency, but basically they are aesthetic in nature (see Premack 1984 for a preliminary account of the relation between pedagogy and aesthetics). The child is trained to conform to a style of speaking, eating, dressing, working, and behaving socially by individuals whose immediate lot is not materially advanced by the child's acquisition of these skills. Chimpanzees approximate this way of behaving. They actually train one another, as few nonhuman species do, but their training is not with pedagogic intent.

For instance, one animal may teach another a sign that was taught it, just as a child whose father tickled it or playfully blew on its cheek may later tickle or blow on the cheek of another child. This is not pedagogy but a form of delayed social imitation. Or the training may provide the trainer immediate benefit. For instance, an animal too short to reach a drinking fountain will train a taller animal to press the button for her. We do not find one animal training another (in a manner that was not just recently imposed on it) for the sake of achieving an ideal form, a form, moreover, that is of no direct benefit to the trainer (Premack 1984). So in chimpanzees, we find training but not pedagogic training. In nonprimates we do not find training of any kind. Nearly all skills acquired by nonprimates are based merely on learning and/or imitation (see Galef 1981 for a review of social transmission in nonhuman mammals). The individual imitated is a passive model who does not have the imitator in mind and provides no feedback to him. Of course, social feedback per se is not confined to humans. If a rat or ape bites or strikes another, there will be feedback. But only in the human could this feedback consist of the instruction to strike the blow more effectively or artistically. In humans, two heads evaluate excellence, and one of them belongs to an expert.

Contributing to pedagogy is social attribution, the disposition to attribute beliefs and intentions to others, a disposition that is highly elaborated in humans. Apes show limited social attribution, approaching in some respects that of the three-and-a-half-year-old child. Both ape and child of this age appear to attribute belief and intention to others, but only insofar as the beliefs are the same as their own. Not until the child is about four years old does he attribute to others beliefs that are different from his own (Winner and Perner 1983). We have not yet found that the ape can take this step (Premack and Premack 1983). The difference is not inconsequential. In one case, you can solve problems on the basis of what you know; in the other case, on the basis of what you know and believe others to know. Moreover, deception is not a possibility if, beyond representing what you know, you cannot also represent what you want someone else to "know." Finally, how astute a pedagogue could you be if you were unable to distinguish between what you know and what you believe someone else knows?

Consciousness, though not itself a social disposition, enables a linkage between humans that is of a "social" kind. When a human not only solves a problem but also becomes conscious of how he did so, he can communicate this knowledge to another, sometimes enabling the latter to do something he could not do alone. For instance, four-year-old children do not induce the semantic concepts of agent, recipient, and instrument of the action from simple visual exemplars. Yet when given explicit definitions of these concepts, they can recognize an indefinite number of examples of them. But what is the source of the explicit definitions? Can we simply look them up in a book? Ultimately, yes, though they depend in the first place on someone's having become conscious of "what an X is," that is, "conscious" of the criterion he uses in treating all Xs as belonging to a category.

Who benefits most from the discovery of how a problem can be solved? Our example suggests not the individual who makes the discovery so much as other members of his group. Recall the study on semantic markers in which the children failed until given explicit definitions. The adult who provided the children with the explicit definitions did not necessarily require them himself; he may have been able to respond correctly before discovering how. The children, on the other hand, could not have responded correctly without having been told how. Some will not discover how they solve a problem until after having found its solution. But the conscious solution of problems on the part of these individuals is a prerequisite to the problem-solving of others. Consciousness may contribute, in this way, to pedagogy, becoming part of the force that binds not only humans to one another, but also one generation to another. The human may be as far removed from the ape in consciousness and metacognition as he is in language (see Flavell 1978 for a review of metacognition in children). These competences may be among the last to have evolved in our species.

Too often these unique social dispositions linking one human with another are confused with language because they are so acutely realized through language (consider the interweaving between human pedagogy and language). But they are dispositions in their own right and lie outside of language. We can conceive of hypothetical species (that do and do not have language) having human social specialization; language would affect only the efficiency of the pedagogy. Conversely, we can conceive of species (that do and do not have social specialization) having human language or discursive representation of comparable power. The simplest way to rationalize language has been as an instrument for consummating unique human social dispositions. However, language is not the only, or even necessarily the major, human specialization. Pedagogy, aesthetics, cognition, social attribution, and consciousness, like language, are some of the major human specializations. To get on with an understanding of our species, we shall have to relinquish our infatuation with language and stop reading and writing papers like the present one.

Appendix

Table 1
Testing for social cues. Number of correct responses/number of trials.

	Trainer A		Trainer B	
	Control	No control	Control	No control
Object matching	19/20	20/20	18/20	19/20
Number matching	13/20	8/20	10/20	9/20

Bibliography

Armstrong, S., Gleitman, L. R., and Gleitman, H. (1983) What some concepts might not be. *Cognition, 13,* 263–308.

Bates, E. (1979) *The emergence of symbols: Cognition and communication in infancy.* New York: Academic Press.

Beer, C. (1976) Some complexities in the communication behavior of gulls. *Annals of the New York Academy of Sciences, 280,* 413–432.

Bellugi, U., and Klima, E. (1966) Syntactic regularities in the speech of children. In J. Lyons and R. Wales (eds.), *Psycholinguistic papers.* Edinburgh: Edinburgh University Press.

Bennett, J. (1976) *Linguistic behavior.* Cambridge: Cambridge University Press.

Bertalanffy, L. von (1968) *General System Theory.* New York: Braziller.

Bickerton, D. (1984) The language bioprogram hypothesis. *The Behavioral and Brain Sciences, 7,* 173–221.

Bitterman, M. (1975) The comparative analysis of learning. *Science, 188,* 699–709.

Bitterman, M. E. (1976) Incentive contrast in honey bees. *Science, 192,* 380–382.

Bloom, L. (1973) *One word at a time.* The Hague: Mouton.

Bloom, L. (1974) Talking, understanding, and thinking. In *Language perspectives: Acquisition, retardation, and intervention.* Baltimore: University Park Press.

Bloom, L., Rocissano, L., and Hood, L. (1976) Adult-child discourse: Developmental interaction between information processing and linguistic knowledge. *Cognitive Psychology, 8,* 521–552.

Bower, T. G. R. (1974) *Development in infancy.* San Francisco: Freeman.

Bowerman, M. (1983) Reorganizational processes in lexical and syntactic development. In E. Wanner and L. Gleitman (eds.), *Language acquisition: The state of the art.* Cambridge: Cambridge University Press.

Bresnan, J. (1978) A realistic transformational grammar. In M. Halle, J. Bresnan, and G. A. Miller (eds.), *Linguistic theory and psychological reality*. Cambridge, MA: The MIT Press.

Brewer, W. F. (1974) There is no convincing evidence for operant or classical conditioning in human adults. In W. Weiner and D. Palermo (eds.), *Cognition and Symbolic Processes*. Hillsdale, NJ: Erlbaum Press.

Brown, R. (1968) The development of Wh questions in child speech. *Journal of Verbal Learning and Verbal Behavior*, 7, 279–290.

Bruner, J. S. (1975) The ontogenesis of speech acts. *Journal of Child Language*, 2, 1–19.

Carew, T. J., Walters, E. T., and Kandel, E. R. (1981) Associative learning in *Aplysia*: cellular correlates supporting a conditioned fear hypthesis. *Science*, 211, 501–503.

Cerella, J. (1982) Mechanisms of concept formation in the pigeon. In D. J. Ingle, M. A. Goodale and R. J. W. Mansfield (eds.), *Analysis of visual behavior*. Cambridge, MA: The MIT Press.

Cheney, D. L., and Seyfarth, R. M. (1982) How vervet monkeys perceive their grunts: Field playback experiments. *Animal Behaviour*, 30, 737–751.

Cheng, K., and Gallistel, C. R. (1984) Testing the geometric power of an animal's spatial representation. In H. Roitblat, T. G. Bever, and H. Terrace (eds.), *Animal Cognition*. Hillsdale, NJ: Erlbaum.

Chevalier-Skolnikoff, S. (1977) The ontogeny of primate intelligence: Implications for communicative potential. In S. Harnad, H. Steklis, and J. Lancaster (eds.), *Origins of language and speech*. New York: New York Academy of Sciences.

Chomsky, N. (1965) *Aspects of the theory of syntax*. Cambridge, MA: The MIT Press.

Chomsky, N. (1980) *Rules and representations*. New York: Columbia University Press.

Danto, A. C. (1983) Images, labels, concepts, and propositions: Some reservations regarding Premack's "abstract code." *The Behavioral and Brain Sciences*, 6, 143–144.

Dennett, D. C. (1971) Intentional systems. *The Journal of Philosophy*, 68, 87–106.

Dickinson, A. (1980) *Contemporary animal learning theory*. Cambridge: Cambridge University Press.

Dobzhansky, T. (1955) *Evolution, genetics and man*. New York: Wiley and Sons, Inc.

Dolgin, K. G. (1981) A developmental study of cognitive predisposition: A study of the relative salience of form and function in adult and four-year-old subjects. Dissertation, University of Pennsylvania.

Estes, W. K. (1969) New perspectives on some old issues in association theory. In N. J. MacKintosh and W. K. Honig (eds.), *Fundamental issues in associative learning*. Halifax, NS: Dalhousie University Press.

Estes, W. K., and Lauer, D. W. (1957) Conditions of invariance and modifiability in simple reversal learning. *Journal of Comparative and Physiological Psychology*, 50, 199–206.

Fischer, S. (1978) Sign language and creoles. In P. Siple (ed.), *Understanding language through sign language research*. New York: Academic Press.

Flavell, J. H. (1978) Metacognitive development. In J. M. Scandura and C. J. Brainerd (eds.), *Structural-process theories of complex human behavior*. Alphen a. d. Rijn, The Netherlands: Sijthoff and Noordhoff.

Fodor, J. A. (1966) How to learn to talk: Some simple ways. In F. L. Smith and G. A. Miller (eds.), *The genesis of language*. Cambridge, MA: The MIT Press.

Fodor, J. A. (1983) *The modularity of mind*. Cambridge, MA: The MIT Press.

Fowler, A. E. (1984) The acquisition of syntax in Down's Syndrome children. Dissertation, University of Pennsylvania.

Galef, B. G. Jr. (1981) The ecology of weaning. In D. J. Gubernick and P. H. Klopfer (eds.), *Parental care in mammals*. New York: Plenum.

Gardner, B. T., and Gardner, R. A. (1975) Evidence for sentence constituents in the early utterances of child and chimpanzee. *Journal of Experimental Psychology: General, 104*, 244–267.

Gardner, B. T., and Gardner, R. A. (1971) Two-way communication with an infant chimpanzee. In A. Schrier and F. Stollnitz (eds.), *Behavior in nonhuman primates*, Vol. 4. New York: Academic Press.

Gelman, R., and Gallistel, C. R. (1978) *The child's understanding of number*. Cambridge, MA: Harvard University Press.

Gillan, D. J., Premack, D., and Woodruff, G. (1981) Reasoning in the chimpanzee: I. Analogical reasoning. *Journal of Experimental Psychology: Animal Behavior Processes, 7*, 1–17.

Gleitman, L. R., and Wanner, E. (1983) Language acquisition: The state of the art. In *Language acquisition: The state of the art*, Cambridge: Cambridge University Press.

Goodman, N. (1965) *Fact, fiction and forecast*, 2nd. ed. Indianapolis: Bobbs-Merrill.

Greenfield, P., and Smith, J. (1976) *The structure of communication in early language development*. New York: Academic Press.

Grice, H. (1975) Logic and conversation. In P. Cole and J. L. Morgan (eds.), *Syntax and semantics*. New York: Academic Press.

Griffin, D. R. (1976) *The question of animal awareness*. New York: Rockefeller University Press.

Guess, D., and Baer, D. M. (1973) An analysis of individual differences in generalization between receptive and productive language in retarded children. *Journal of Applied Behavior Analysis, 6*, 311–329.

Haber, L. (1983) Language training versus training in relations. *The Behavioral and Brain Sciences, 6*, 146–147.

Harlow, H. F. (1949) The formation of learning sets. *Psychological Review, 56*, 51–65.

Hayes, C. (1951) *The ape in our house.* New York: Harper.

Hayes, K. J., Thompson, R., and Hayes, C. (1953) Current discrimination learning in chimpanzees. *Journal of Comparative and Physiological Psychology, 46*, 105–107.

Hayes, K. J., and Nissen, C. H. (1971) Higher mental functions of a home-raised chimpanzee. In A. M. Schrier and F. Stollnitz (eds.), *Behavior of nonhuman primates*, Vol. 4. New York: Academic Press.

Hebb, D. O., and Thompson, W. R. (1976) The social significance of animal studies. In G. Lindsey and E. Aronson (eds.), *The handbook of social psychology*, 2nd ed., Vol. II, *Research Methods.* Reading, MA: Addison-Wesley.

Hempel, C. G. (1965) *Aspects of scientific explanation.* New York: Free Press, Collier-Macmillan.

Herman, L. M., Richards, D. G., and Wolz, J. P. (1984) Comprehension of sentences by Bottlenosed Dolphins. *Cognition, 16*, 129–219.

Herrnstein, R., Loveland, D., and Cable, P. (1976) Natural concepts in pigeons. *Journal of Experimental Psychology: Animal Behavior Processes, 2*, 285–302.

Hockett, C. F. (1959) Animal "languages" and human language. In J. N. Spuhler (ed.), *The evolution of man's capacity for culture.* Detroit: Wayne State University Press.

Hockett, C. F. (1960) Logical considerations in the study of animal communication. In W. E. Lanyon and W. N. Tavolga (eds.), *Animal sounds and communication.* Washington, DC: American Institute of Biological Sciences.

Irwin, F. (1971) *Intentional behavior and motivation.* Philadelphia: Lippincott.

Johnson, D. E., and Postal, P. (1980) *Arc-pair grammar.* Princeton: Princeton University Press.

Karmiloff-Smith, A. (1979) Micro- and macrodevelopmental changes in language acquisition and other representational systems. *Cognitive Science, 3*, 91–118.

Klima, E. (1975) Sound and its absence in the linguistic symbol. In J. F. Kavanagh and J. E. Cutting (eds.), *The role of speech in language.* Cambridge, MA: The MIT Press.

Klima, E., and Bellugi, U. (1979) *The sign of language.* Cambridge, MA: Harvard University Press.

Köhler, W. (1925) *The mentality of apes.* London: Kegan.

Kuhl, P. K., and Miller, J. C. (1975) Speech perception by the chinchilla: voiced–voiceless distinction in alveolar plosive consonants. *Science, 190,* 69–72.

Labov, W. Intensity. Paper given at Georgetown Round Table, 15 March 1984.

Lenneberg, E. H. (1967) *Biological foundations of language.* New York: Wiley.

Lieberman, P. (1985) *The biology and evolution of language.* Cambridge, MA: Harvard University Press.

Lieberman, P. (1975) The evolution of speech and language. In J. F. Kavanagh and J. E. Cutting (eds.), *The role of speech in language.* Cambridge, MA: The MIT Press.

Lieberman, P. (1973) On the evolution of human language: a unified view. *Cognition, 2,* 59–94.

MacCorquodale, K., Meehl, P. E. and Tolman, E. C. (1954). In W. K. Estes, S. Koch, K. MacCorquodale, P. E. Meehl, C. G. Mueller, W. N. Schoenfeld, and W. S. Verplanck (eds.), *Modern learning theory.* New York: Appleton-Century-Crofts.

Markman, E. M. (1983) The acquisition and hierarchical organization of categories by children. Paper prepared for the Carnegie Symposium on Cognition.

McClure, M., Gillan, D. J., Woodruff, G., Thompson, R., and Premack, D. Comparison of "natural reasoning" in children and chimpanzees. In preparation.

McNeill, D. (1974) Sentence structure in chimpanzee communication. In K. J. Connolly and J. S. Bruner (eds.), *The growth of competence.* New York: Academic Press.

Mehler, J., and Bertoncini, J. (1981) Syllables as units in infant perception, *Infant Behavior and Development, IV,* 271–284.

Menzel, E. W. (1973) Chimpanzee spatial memory organization. *Science, 182,* 943–945.

Miles, H. L. Apes and language: The search for communicative competence. In J. de Luce and H. T. Wilder (eds.), *Language in Primates: Implications for linguistics, anthropology, psychology and philosophy.* Bloomington, IN: Indiana University Press, forthcoming.

Miller, G. A. (1981) *Language and speech.* San Francisco: W. H. Freeman.

Miller, G. A., and Chomsky, N. (1963) Finitary models of language users. In R. Bush, D. Luce, and E. Galanter (eds.), *Readings in mathematical psychology.* New York: Wiley.

Miller, G. A., and Johnson-Laird, P. N. (1976) *Language and perception.* Cambridge, MA: Harvard University Press.

Morris, C. W. (1946) *Signs, language, and behavior.* New York: Prentice-Hall.

Moynihan, M. H. (1970) Control, suppression, decay, disappearance and replacement of displays. *Journal of Theoretical Biology, 29,* 85–112.

Newport, E. L. (1983) Task specificity in language learning? Evidence from speech perception and American Sign Language. In E. Wanner and L. R. Gleitman (eds.), *Language acquisition: The state of the art.* Cambridge: Cambridge University Press.

Newport, E. L., and Supalla, T. The structuring of language: clues from the acquisition of signed and spoken language. In U. Bellugi and M. Studdert-Kennedy (eds.), *Signed and spoken language: biological constraints on linguistic form.* Dahlem Konferenzen. Weinheim Verlag Chemie.

Pasnak, R. (1979) Acquisition of prerequisites to conservation by macaques. *Journal of Experimental Psychology: Animal Behavior Processes, 5,* 194–210.

Passingham, R. (1982) *The human primate.* San Fancisco: W. H. Freeman.

Patterson, F. (1978) Conversations with a gorilla. *National Geographic, 154,* 438–465.

Perlmutter, D. M. (1980) Relational grammar. In E. Moravcsik and J. Wirth (eds.), *Syntax and semantics. Vol. 13. Current approaches to syntax.* New York: Academic Press.

Piatelli-Palmarini, M. (ed.) (1980) *Language and learning.* Cambridge, MA: Harvard University Press.

Plooij, F. X. (1978) Some basic traits of language in wild chimpanzees? In A. Lock (ed.), *Action, gesture, and symbol.* New York: Academic Press.

Popper, K. (1972) *The logic of scientific discovery.* New York: Hutchinson.

Premack, D. (1983) The codes of man and beasts. *The Behavioral and Brain Sciences, 6,* 125–167.

Premack, D. (1976) *Intelligence in ape and man.* Hillsdale, NJ: Erlbaum.

Premack, D. (1971) Language in chimpanzee? *Science, 172,* 808–822.

Premack, D. (1984) Pedagogy and aesthetics as sources of culture. In M. S. Gazzaniga (ed.), *Handbook of cognitive neuroscience.* New York: Plenum Press.

Premack, D. (1975) Putting a face together. *Science, 188,* 228–236.

Premack, D., and Premack, A. J. (1983) *The mind of an ape.* New York: Norton.

Premack, D., and Schwartz, A. (1966) Preparations for discussing behaviorism with chimpanzee. In F. L. Smith and G. A. Miller (eds.), *The genesis of language.* Cambridge, MA: The MIT Press.

Premack, D., and Woodruff, G. (1978) Does the chimpanzee have a theory of mind? *The Behavioral and Brain Sciences, 4,* 515–526.

Putnam, H. (1975) The meaning of meaning. In K. Gunderson (ed.), *Minnesota Studies in the Philosophy of Sciences, Vol. 7.* Minneapolis: University of Minnesota Press.

Pylyshyn, Z. (1980) Computation and cognition: Issues in the foundations of cognitive science. *Behavior and Brain Sciences*, *3*, 111–132.

Quine, W. V. (1973) On the reasons for indeterminacy of translation. *The Journal of Philosophy*, 178–183.

Quine, W. V. (1960) *Word and object*. Cambridge, MA: The MIT Press.

Rescorla, R. A., and Wagner, A. R. (1972) A theory of Pavlovian conditioning: variations in the effectiveness of reinforcement and nonreinforcement. In A. Black and W. F. Prokasy (eds.), *Classical Conditioning II*. New York: Appleton-Century-Crofts.

Reynolds, P. C. (1972) Play, language, and human evolution. Paper presented at 1972 meeting of American Association for Advancement of Science, Washington, DC.

Rosch, E. (1975) Cognitive representations of semantic categories. *Journal of Experimental Psychology: General*, *104*, 192–233.

Rozin, P. (1976) The evolution of intelligence and access to the cognitve unconscious. *Progression in Psychobiology and Physiological Psychology*, *6*, 245–280.

Russell, B. (1940) *An inquiry into meaning and truth*. London: Allen and Unwin Ltd.

Sanders, R. J. (1980) The influence of verbal and nonverbal context on the sign language conversations of a chimpanzee. Dissertation, Columbia University.

Sankoff, G. (1980) Variation, pidgins and creoles. In A. Valdman and A. Highfield (eds.), *Theoretical orientations in creole studies*. New York: Academic Press.

Savage-Rumbaugh, E. S., and Rumbaugh, D. M. (1978) Symbolization, language, and chimpanzees: A theoretical reevaluation based on initial language acquisition processes in four young Pan troglodytes. *Brain and Language*, *6*, 265–300.

Schwartz, R. (1980) How rich a theory of mind? *The Behavioral and Brain Sciences*, *3*, 616–618.

Schusterman, R., and Krieger, K. (1984) California sea lions are capable of semantic comprehension. *The Psychological Record*, *34*, 3–23.

Seidenberg, M. S., and Petitio, L. A. (1979) Signing behavior in apes: A critical review. *Cognition*, *7*, 177–215.

Skinner, B. F. (1935) The generic nature of the concepts of stimulus and response. *Journal of General Psychology*, *12*, 40–65.

Slobin, D. I. (1977) Language change in childhood and in history. In J. Macnamara (ed.), *Language, learning and thought*. New York: Academic Press.

Slobin, D. I. (1983) Preconditions for language acquisition. In E. Wanner and L. R. Gleitman (eds.), *Language acquisition: The state of the art*. Cambridge: Cambridge University Press.

Slobin, D. I. (1979) *Psycholinguistics*, 2nd ed. Glenview, IL: Scott, Foresman.

Smith, E. E., and Medin, D. I. (1981) *Categories and concepts*. Cambridge, MA: Harvard University Press.

Spearman, C. (1937) *Psychology down the ages*. London: Macmillan.

Spelke, E. S. (1982) Perceptual knowledge of objects in infancy. In J. Mehler, M. F. Garrett, and E. C. Walker (eds.), *Perspectives in mental representation*. Hillsdale, NJ: Erlbaum.

Spiker, C. C. (1956) Stimulus pretraining and subsequent performance in the delayed reaction experiments. *Jounal of Experimental Psychology*, *52*, 107–111.

Struhsaker, T. T. (1967) Auditory communication among vervet monkeys. In S. A. Altman (ed.), *Social communication among primates*. Chicago: University of Chicago Press.

Terrace, H. S., Petitio, L. A., Sanders, R. J., and Bever, T. G. (1979) Can an ape create a sentence? *Science*, *206*, 891–900.

Thompson, R. K. R., and Herman, L. M. (1977) Memory for lists of sounds by the bottle-nosed dolphin: Convergence of memory processes with humans? *Science*, *195*, 501–503.

Tolman, E. C. (1932) *Purposive behavior in animals and men*. New York: Century, 1932.

Wanner, E., and Maratsos, M. (1978) An ATN approach to comprehension. In M. Halle, J. Bresnan, and G. A. Miller (eds.), *Linguistic theory and psychological reality*. Cambridge, MA: The MIT Press.

Waters, R. S., and Wilson, W. A. (1976) Speech perception by rhesus monkeys: The voicing distinction in synthesized labial and velar stop consonants. *Perception and Psychophysics*, *19*, 285–289.

Wexler, K., and Culicover, P. (1980) *Formal principles of language acquisition*. Cambridge, MA: The MIT Press.

Winner, H., and Perner, J. (1983) Beliefs about beliefs: Representation and constraining function of wrong beliefs in young children's understanding of deception. *Cognition*, *13*, 103–128.

Woodruff, G., and Premack, D. (1979) Intentional communication in the chimpanzee: The development of deception. *Cognition*, *7*, 333–362.

Woodruff, G., and Premack, D. (1981) Primitive mathematical concepts in the chimpanzee: Proportionality and numerosity. *Nature*, *293*, 568–570.